GLOBETROTTER

Travel

JAPAN

SUE THOMPSON

NEW
HOLLAND

NEW HOLLAND

★★★ Highly recommended
★★ Recommended
★ See if you can

Fifth edition published in 2011
by New Holland Publishers (UK) Ltd
London • Cape Town • Sydney • Auckland
10 9 8 7 6 5 4 3 2 1

website: www.newhollandpublishers.com

Garfield House, 86 Edgware Road
London W2 2EA, United Kingdom

80 McKenzie Street
Cape Town 8001, South Africa

Unit 1, 66 Gibbes Street,
Chatswood NSW 2067, Australia

218 Lake Road
Northcote, Auckland, New Zealand

Distributed in the USA by
The Globe Pequot Press, Connecticut

ISBN 978 1 84773 862 2

This guidebook has been written by independent authors and
updaters. The information therein represents their impartial
opinion, and neither they nor the publishers accept payment
in return for including in the book or writing more favourable
reviews of any of the establishments. Whilst every effort has
been made to ensure that this guidebook is as accurate and
up to date as possible, please be aware that the facts quoted
are subject to change, particularly the price of food, transport
and accommodation. The Publisher accepts no responsibility
or liability for any loss, injury or inconvenience incurred by
readers or travellers using this guide.

Acknowledgements:
The author would like to thank the Japan National Tourist
Organization for its invaluable assistance with travel arrange-
ments and information, as well as Sue Tachibana, Jonathan
Smith and Christian Wignall for their help.

Dedication:
In memory of Bruce Herrod for his photographs of Tokyo,
taken shortly before his death on the First South African
Everest Expedition in 1996.

Publishing Manager: Thea Grobbelaar
DTP Cartographic Manager: Genené Hart
Editors: Carla Redelinghuys, Lorissa Bouwer, Alicha van Reenen,
Melany McCallum, Ingrid Schneider
Consultant: Nigel Hicks
Updated by: Jane Anson
Design and DTP: Nicole Bannister, Lellyn Creamer
Cartographers: Nicole Bannister, Inga Ndibongo, Reneé
Spocter, Tanja Spinola, Genené Hart
Picture Researcher: Shavonne Govender
Reproduction by Hirt & Carter (Pty) Ltd, Cape Town
Printed and bound by Times Offset (M) Sdn. Bhd., Malaysia.

Photographic credits:
Axiom/Paul Quayle: pages 39, 54, 103; **Axiom/Jim Holmes:**
pages 107, 110, 115, 117, 119; **Bigpiepictures/Nicholas
Sumner:** pages 17, 82, 95; **ffotograff/Suzanne Greenslade:**
pages 93, 94; **ffotograff/Nick Turner:** pages 64, 78;
GI/TSI/David Ball: page 10; **GI/TSI/Rex A Butcher:** page 70;
GI/TSI/Wayne Eastep: title page; **GI/TSI/Charles Gupton:** page
29 (bottom); **GI/TSI/Gavin Hellier:** page 69; **GI/TSI/Joel Rogers:**
page 4; **GI/TSW:** page 104; **GI/TSW/Nicholas DeVore:** page
26; **Paul Harris:** page 71; **Bruce Herrod:** pages 18, 22, 25, 30,
33, 34, 36, 37, 38, 42, 66, 67; **HL:** page 29 (top); **HL/Jon
Burbank:** pages 8, 9, 11, 16, 28, 83, 116; **HL/Robert Francis:**
page 90; **HL/JG Fuller:** page 27; **HL/Michael Macintyre:** pages
12, 13, 14, 15, 89; **Look/Hauke Dressler:** pages 72, 74, 75;
Look/Rainer Martini: page 100; **Eric Nathan:** pages 23, 24, 40;
Pictures Colour Library: cover; **Neil Setchfield:** page 21; **Jeroen
Snijders:** pages 20, 58, 81, 91, 106; **Sue Thompson:** pages 6, 7,
19, 45, 46, 50, 53, 55, 57, 59, 60, 73, 84, 86, 87, 98, 112.
GI/TSI = *Gallo Images/Tony Stone Images*
GI/TSW = *Gallo Images/Tony Stone Worldwide*
HL = *Hutchison Library*

Keep us Current
Information in travel guides is apt to change, which is why
we regularly update our guides. We'd be grateful to receive
feedback if you've noted something we should include in our
updates. If you have new information, please share it with us
by writing to the Publishing Manager, Globetrotter, at the
office nearest to you (addresses on this page). The most
significant contribution to each new edition will receive a
free copy of the updated guide.

Cover: *Mount Fuji and Lake Kawaguchi.*
Title Page: *Young Japanese schoolgirls on a sightseeing trip,
crossing stepping stones on a pond.*

CONTENTS

1
Introducing Japan

From subtropical Okinawa to subarctic Hokkaidō, the population of Japan packs itself into an area smaller than California, under the nominal rule of an emperor traditionally descended from Amaterasu, the sun goddess. In a landscape graced by **natural seasonal beauty** and marred by eye-searing **urban meltdown**, geography, mythology and history fuse in a **rich cultural heritage** of arts, crafts and festivals rivalled by a modern-day religious reverence for trends, gadgets and gizmos.

The heartland of Japanese civilization, the island of **Honshū** boasts the top cultural attractions: aristocratic Japan lurks in the temples and villas of **Nara**, **Kyoto** and **Kanazawa**; feudal Japan is embodied in the majesty of **Himeji Castle** and the Zen temples of **Kamakura**; scenic Japan lies in the mountains and national parks, while cutting-edge Japan forges ahead in the skyscrapers, shops and restaurants of Tokyo and Yokohama.

Of the other main islands, **Hokkaidō** is Japan's final frontier and the best skiing destination; **Shikoku** is a low-key place to enjoy local festivals and cuisine, and **Kyūshū** is Japan's gateway to Asia, with rugged coastal scenery, hot springs and strong mythological associations.

The Japanese love to travel within their own country; group tours are as much an institution here as Mount Fuji. But with a little bit of imagination and patience, it is possible to experience the magic of Japan unpackaged. The low crime rate, **excellent rail system** and people generally forgiving of foreign habits make Japan a wonderful country to explore.

Opposite: *Japanese gardens have an air of antiquity and seclusion.*

WHAT TO DO IN AN EARTHQUAKE

• Switch off the gas supply and all electrical appliances.
• Open all the doors to prevent jamming.
• Stay away from glass/heavy objects. Preferably stand in a ground floor doorway or crouch under a table.
• At night, have a torch to hand. Know the location of emergency exits in your hotel.
• When the tremors have died down proceed to the nearest open space/designated emergency centre.
• If in a car, stop immediately. Switch off engine and try to take shelter.
• Get in touch with your embassy as soon as possible.

Opposite: *Boreal forest dominates the mountainous wilds of Hokkaidō.*
Below: *The tranquil shores of the volcanic crater lake at Osore-zan are the antithesis of the seismic activity that formed them.*

THE LAND

The Shinto gods Izanami and Izanagi had their work cut out for them when they gave birth to Japan. Down to the smallest pine-studded rock, the archipelago comprises around 3000 islands separated from the rim of the Asian continent by the Sea of Okhotsk, the Sea of Japan and the East China Sea.

The four main islands span approximately 1600km (994 miles): **Honshū** is roughly comparable in size to the UK; **Hokkaidō** to Scotland; **Shikoku** to Wales and **Kyūshū** to Switzerland. The northernmost point of Hokkaidō, at 45°31'N, lies parallel with Montreal. Yonaguni-jima, in the Yaeyama Islands, is on virtually the same latitude as the Bahamas; at 122°55'E, it is also Japan's westernmost point.

Volcanic and Seismic Activity

Japan sits uncomfortably at the junction of three major **tectonic** plates: the Eurasian plate to the west, the Philippine plate to the south and the Pacific plate to the east. Off the eastern edge of the archipelago, where these plates collide, lie a series of **marine trenches** plunging to depths of 9000m (29,500ft).

Japan is a permanent hot bed of **volcanic and seismic activity**. Over 80 volcanoes are now classified as active, among them Mount Fuji – even though it has not erupted since 1707. Low-level earth tremors are common, but nature can and does unleash strong **earthquakes**, as the port city of **Kōbe** found to its cost in 1995.

Geothermal Springs

An altogether more benign product of the geological cauldron boiling beneath the archipelago is the plethora of **geothermal springs** (*onsen*), in which the Japanese have bathed for centuries. *Onsen* all over the country are classified according to mineral content, which determines therapeutic value. Kyūshū is famous for its sand and mud baths.

Mountains and Forests

Three quarters of Japan is **mountainous** and two thirds is **heavily forested**. Six intersecting mountain arcs, soaring to elevations of over 3000m (9843ft) in the Japan Alps, separate the country into two sections: one faces the Sea of Japan; the other faces the Pacific. Dividing the mountains are deep valleys, gorges, lakes and plunging waterfalls.

Forest cover is varied; conifers predominate in Hokkaidō, whereas deciduous trees such as maple, oak and ash, as well as conifers, cover much of northern Honshū. Subtropical evergreens such as laurel and camphor are found in Kyūshū and Shikoku.

Plains

Alluvial **plains and plateaux** (approximately 25% of the total landmass) are found mostly on the Pacific Coast, with the notable exception of Niigata. The lack of flat, cultivable land is the main reason why some 80% of the population lives on Honshū and why the Kantō region and the Pacific coast bear the brunt of urban development. Central and northern Honshū, as well as southern Kyūshū and Shikoku are relatively sparsely populated. So is Hokkaidō, the centre of Japan's dairy farming industry.

GEOGRAPHICAL FACTS AND FIGURES

Land mass: 377,873km² (145,859 sq miles).
Principal divisions: 47 prefectures (including metropolitan areas).
Length of main archipelago: approximately 1600km (994 miles).
Largest plain: Kantō, 15,000km² (5790 sq miles).
Highest mountain: Mount Fuji, 3776m (12,389ft).
Biggest lake: Biwa, 674km² (260 sq miles).
Population: 127,078,679 million (July 2009 estimate).

COMPARATIVE CLIMATE CHART	SAPPORO				TOKYO				KAGOSHIMA			
	WIN	SPR	SUM	AUT	WIN	SPR	SUM	AUT	WIN	SPR	SUM	AUT
	JAN	APR	JULY	OCT	JAN	APR	JULY	OCT	JAN	APR	JULY	OCT
MIN TEMP. °C	-8	2	17	6	1	10	22	14	3	12	24	15
MAX TEMP. °C	-1	11	25	16	10	18	29	21	12	21	31	25
MIN TEMP. °F	18	36	63	43	34	50	72	57	37	54	75	59
MAX TEMP. °F	30	52	77	61	50	64	84	70	54	70	88	77
RAINFALL mm	107	62	69	116	45	125	126	164	87	230	304	106
RAINFALL in	4	2	3	5	2	5	5	6	3	9	12	4
DAYS OF RAINFALL	21	9	12	14	2	10	13	6	5	9	13	6

Above: *Admiring the magnificent cherry blossoms along the Imperial Palace moat in Tokyo is an established ritual.*
Opposite: *Maple trees in Kyoto, ablaze with the fiery colours of autumn.*

Sea Coast

As a result of fault lines running parallel to the seaboard, the coast along the Sea of Japan is less rugged than the Pacific Coast. On the Pacific side, where fault lines intersect at angles, there are numerous rocky bays and inlets. This is also true of the western coast of Kyūshū. The **Inland Sea** (Seto Naikai), on the other hand, is dotted with countless scenic islands.

Climate

Japan has **very distinct seasons** and huge **temperature extremes**. Proximity to the eastern seaboard of the Asian land mass subjects the archipelago to the cold northwesterly monsoon in winter and, in summer, to the warm, moist air of the southeasterly monsoon.

From the first signs of winter to the arrival of **cherry blossoms** in spring, Japanese weather forecasting is the stuff of religious ritual, dished out in tedious detail on nightly television bulletins. Each flower has its own seasonal slot; each season has its own gift-giving rituals, and inspires its own literature.

SEASONAL SPLENDOUR

February–March: plum, camellia
March–April: camellia, cherry, magnolia
May–June: azalea, wisteria, peony, iris, water lily
July: lotus
September: bush clover
October: maple leaves
November: chrysanthemums

Seasons

From November, cold northwesterlies bring prodigious amounts of **snow** to northern Honshū, the Sea of Japan coast, the Japan Alps and Hokkaidō, parts of which remain snowbound until late April. The Sea of Okhotsk off the east coast of Hokkaidō freezes over, while the Pacific coast rarely sees much snow.

Late February heralds the arrival of **spring** on Honshū. The weather tends to be mild but rainy, until clearer skies bring on the cherry blossom season, which starts in February in Okinawa and ripples through Honshū from late March, reaching Hokkaidō in early May. Temperatures and humidity begin to rise.

Summer begins with the **baiu,** or **tsuyu** (plum rains), which start to fall in early June in the southern and western parts of Japan. Hokkaidō escapes virtually unscathed. By late June, Kyūshū is usually in the grip of heavy rains and often suffers landslides and flooding. As the southeasterly monsoon takes over, the air turns very humid and sticky.

In late August and September, the **shūrin** (long autumn rains) set in, bringing precipitation to Hokkaidō and **typhoons** to Kyūshū, Shikoku and even the Kantō plain. **Autumn** is short; days are mild and sunny. This is the most popular time to get out and see the **maple leaves**, which make Hokkaidō resemble New England in October. By November, Honshū is resplendent in autumn colours.

Flora and Fauna

In July and August, **alpine flowers** bloom in the Northern Alps of Central Honshū and Daisetsuzan National Park in Hokkaidō. The area around Hakuba in Nagano Prefecture is particularly well known for its rare varieties.

Japan has some 490 species of birds ranging from exotica such as **Blakiston's Fish Owl** (*Ketupa blakistoni*) and the graceful **Japanese Crane** (*Grus japonensis müllar*) to the **ptarmigan** (found in alpine zones) and the **pheasant**, which is the national bird.

The archipelago has around 100 species of land mammals. The largest is the **Hokkaidō brown bear** (*Ursus arctos yesoensis*). Smaller, more commonly seen species include the fox, the **tanuki** (a type of racoon), and macaque monkeys, which look their cutest – from a distance – when they are bathing in hot pools surrounded by snow. Japan's rarest species is the **wild cat**, which is found on **Iriomote Island** in the

TYPHOONS

The word typhoon, from the Chinese word *tai fung* (great wind), is used to describe tropical storms arising in the Western Pacific in late summer or early autumn. Typhoons are numbered by year and order of formation. Japan's most damaging typhoon in recent history was the **Ise Bay Typhoon** of 26 September 1959, which killed 5000 people and damaged over 1 million buildings. Peak winds reached 45m (49yd) per second. In 2004 an all time high of ten typhoons hit the mainland and Typhoon 23 in Oct 2004 left 94 people dead or missing. In 2009 Typhoon Melor killed 2 people. Winds reached 198km per hour (123 miles per hour). Typhoon warnings are issued by the Meteorological Agency. Once the danger is deemed to be over, a typhoon is downgraded to 'tropical storm' status.

NATIONAL PARKS

Japan established a national park system in the 1930s in recognition of the fact that industrialization threatened its mountains and forests. There are now **28 national parks** across Japan, from the Shiretoko National Park in Hokkaidō to Kirishima-Yaku National Park in Kyūshū. Each park has visitor centres that explain the local environment and wildlife, and give information on hiking trails. The most popular parks, such as Fuji-Hakone-Izu, draw big crowds on weekends and public holidays. It is always worth trying to make a week-day excursion. *See* www.env.go.jp/en/nature/nps/park for details on parks.

Okinawa chain. Japan's deadliest creature is the **habu**, a poisonous snake that also inhabits Okinawa.

Environment

The Japanese do not like to solve their environmental problems in court, as the record shows: complaints about pollution from the **Ashio Copper Mine** in Tochigi Prefecture were first raised in the 1880s, but local farmers did not win compensation until 1974.

Worse still was **Minamata Disease**, which struck thousands of people in southern Kyūshū in the 1950s. Following investigation, it turned out that the paralysis and convulsions were caused by eating fish that had been contaminated with mercury. Again, it took decades to reach a settlement.

Having sacrificed its environment on the altar of industrialization for much of the 20th century, Japan now spends a lot of time and money on **pollution control**, particularly to improve the quality of the water and air. Despite some of the tightest exhaust emission standards in the world, however, Mount Fuji is rarely visible from Tokyo.

HISTORY IN BRIEF

The earliest stone tools found in Japan date back some 50,000 years, to a time when hunter-gatherers inhabited the archipelago. The **Jōmon Period** (10,000–300BC) is named after distinctive 'cord-pattern' pots of the era, not dissimilar to the incised pottery found in China and Manchuria.

Archaeological evidence suggests that the Jōmon people were hunters and fishermen, who lived in settlements and used stone tools and ceramics. Skeletal remains also suggest that they were more closely related to the

Below: *The glory of Mount Fuji seen across Lake Ashi.*

Ainu of Hokkaidō, a people of Caucasian origin, than to the modern Japanese.

The **Yayoi Period** (300BC–AD300) saw the introduction of paddy rice farming and crop cultivation, triggered by waves of migrants from the Korean peninsula to Kyūshū. These people, thought to be the ancestors of the modern Japanese, brought with them bronze and iron implements, as well as weapons and ceremonial objects such as bells.

Above: *The cultivation of rice, Japan's staple food, requires both hard work and excellent irrigation.*

During the early **Kofun** (Tumulus) Era (AD300–710), the chronicles of the Wei Dynasty in China refer to Japan as a land of over 100 separate 'kingdoms' ruled by chieftains. One powerful ruler was the legendary **Himiko**, an Asian version of Queen Boadicea, whose name is now used by a leading Tokyo women's shoe company.

Further waves of migration from Korea brought skilled craftsmen and scribes. By the late 5th century, a dominant society formed of clans (*uji*) and guilds (*be*), had taken definitive shape. Now referred to as the **Yamato** state, it marked a shift in the focus of civilization from Kyūshū to the **Nara** region of central Honshū.

Courtly History

The **Asuka** and **Hakuhō** periods (AD552–710) marked a transition to courtly traditions that were to dominate the next five centuries. The trigger was the introduction, ca. AD552, of Buddhist sculptures and scriptures from the Korean kingdom of Paekche. Subsequently, **Crown Prince Shōtoku** (AD574–622) elevated Buddhism to a state religion. The immense artistic achievements of this period live on in the temple treasures and architecture of **Hōryū-ji**, near modern-day Nara.

The Asuka Period also marked a transition from Korean to Chinese influence, culminating in reforms

HANIWA

The most tangible reminders of the **Kofun** era are the massive key-hole burial mounds (also found in Korea) in north Kyūshū and around Nara. Originally, these mounds were surrounded by *haniwa*, clay pottery figures of varying degrees of sophistication, including warriors and animals. There is no evidence, however, that *haniwa* were used as substitutes for human sacrifice. Tombs have also yielded a variety of bronze mirrors, saddle fittings, curved jewels, belts and crowns similar to objects excavated from burial sites on the Siberian Steppe and Korea.

Above: *The skilful art of 17th-century Bunraku puppetry continues today, with love tragedies an ever-popular theme.*

CHRONICLES AND MYTH

The *Kojiki* (Record of Ancient Matters) tells the 'history' of Japan, beginning with the creation of the Japanese archipelago by the gods **Izanami** and **Izanagi**. It also chronicles the birth of the first, mythical emperor, **Jimmu**, the direct descendant of the Shinto sun goddess, Amaterasu, keeper of the imperial regalia. Jimmu, it is claimed, came to the throne in 600BC, thus making Japan the oldest monarchy in the world. Until 1 January 1946, when Emperor Hirohito renounced his divinity in the wake of Japan's defeat by allied forces, the imperial family's claim to divine origins was based largely on the *Kojiki*.

designed to turn Japan into a fully centralized Tang Dynasty-style bureaucracy. Japan's first Chinese-style capital, laid out on a grid pattern, was built in AD694 at Fujiwara in the Asuka valley.

In AD710 the capital was moved again, this time to **Nara**. Here, via the court's outpost of **Dazaifu** in Kyūshū, splendid gifts of tribute began to arrive from China and Central Asia, many to celebrate the dedication of the **Great Buddha of Tōdai-ji** in AD752.

The **Nara Period** (AD710–794) marked the first major developments in literature: the *Kojiki* (AD712) and *Nihon-shoki* (AD720), both works of history-cum-mythology, and the *Manyō-shū*, an anthology of poetry, appeared, written in a cumbersome system of Chinese characters used to express Japanese (which at that time had no writing system of its own).

Eventually, the power of the Buddhist monasteries was perceived as a threat to the throne. This prompted yet another move in AD794, this time to **Heian-kyō** (modern-day Kyoto).

Heian Period (AD794–1185)

The new capital at **Heian-kyō** was to remain the seat of the imperial household until 1868. The city, modelled on Changan (Xian), the Tang Dynasty capital of China, covered an area of $22km^2$ (8.5 sq miles) and had a population of around 50,000. Top-ranking officials were favoured with land rights in perpetuity. This enabled them to assemble vast estates, which they ran as absentee landlords from their rigidly hierarchical, rarefied world of splendid costumes and poetry contests, as depicted in *The Tale of Genji* and *emaki-mono* (picture scrolls) of the period.

An indomitable family called the **Fujiwara** rose to power at court by marrying its women into the imperial line and ruling as regents over imperial affairs. Lower ranking, impoverished officials often fell subject to factionalism and back-stabbing, and ended up in the provinces – a fate worse than death. One such victim was **Sugawara Michizane** (AD845–903), a brilliant courtier exiled to Dazaifu. After his death he was deified as Kitano Tenjin, patron of learning, at shrines called Tenman-gū. These still exist all over Japan and attract droves of school children.

As the 10th and 11th centuries progressed, unrest in the provinces and famine began to disturb the cocoon of court life. The rise of warrior families, backed by competing aristocratic factions, eventually eclipsed the Fujiwara, except for the northern branch headed by **Fujiwara Kiyohira** (1056–1128). In 1095, Kiyohira set up a lavish court at **Hiraizumi** (*see* page 59), destined to rival Heian-kyō.

By the end of the 12th century, the outcome of a battle between two clans, the **Taira** and **Minamoto**, was to set the stage for nearly 700 years of military rule.

Rule of the *Shōguns*
Kamakura Period (1185–1333)

In 1185, **Minamoto Yoritomo** (1147–99), victor over the Taira at the Battle of Dan-no-ura, established a feudal government (*bakufu*) at Kamakura in eastern Japan. The imperial court at Kyoto was thus reduced to puppet status.

In 1274 and 1281, the *bakufu* deflected two attempted invasions of Kyūshū by the Mongols. On the second occasion, the invaders were beaten back by a typhoon that entered the annals of history as the **kamikaze** (divine wind), the name subsequently given to Japan's suicide pilots in World War II.

> ### THE TALE OF GENJI
>
> In the Heian Period, Chinese was the language of scholars, but much poetry and prose fiction became distinctly 'Japanese'. Written in the newly developed *kana* (syllabic) script, it was often the product of bored noble-women closeted away at court. The most important work is *The Tale of Genji*, by **Murasaki Shikibu**, who picked up her brush around 1000 years ago to write an epic of romance, politics and intrigue, twice as long as *War and Peace*. *The Tale of Genji* has inspired an entire industry of scholarship, modern translations, films and even, in the 1980s, a pop group.

Below: *Antique markets hold untold treasures for bargain hunters.*

THE WAY OF TEA

Tea became popular in Japan in the 12th century, when **Zen monks** returned with powdered tea (*matcha*) from Song-Dynasty China, where it was used to stay awake during meditation. Tea was first grown in Japan at Uji, the aristocratic retreat between Kyoto and Nara. The 14th-century **Ashikaga *shōguns*** became avid tea drinkers. By the 15th century, tea drinking had attained new heights. In the 16th century, the tea ceremony began to evolve, using a simple, rustic *cha-shitsu* (tea room) adorned only with an alcove, scroll and flower arrangement.

Opposite: *Archery contest at Sanjūsangen-dō, Kyoto.*
Below: *Monks of the Sōtō Zen sect at a ceremony.*

There were new developments in religion and art. **Zen Buddhism**, brought back from China by monks, strongly appealed to the warrior classes because of its reliance on self-discipline. A new realism was displayed in sculpture and portrait paintings.

Muromachi Period (1333–1568)

In 1333, the Ashikaga *shōguns* in Kyoto came to power. Trade missions were sent to China and commercial activity began to flourish. The Ashikaga, however, were intrinsically weak. Idly hoping that the bonds of feudalism would hold, they buried themselves in the niceties of **Nō** theatre and poetry but, as they lost control, feudal domains turned to fierce rivalry. The arrival of the Portuguese in the mid-16th century introduced guns and **Christianity**; trade with the Dutch and Chinese followed.

Momoyama Period (1568–1600)

In the late 16th century, three war lords gradually drew Japan back under centralized control. **Oda Nobunaga** (1534–82) began the process of reunification, but was then assassinated. The rabidly anti-Christian **Toyotomi Hideyoshi** (1537–98) then took up the reins. In the 1590s, Hideyoshi launched a series of invasions on Korea, bringing back with him the Korean potters destined to found Japan's porcelain industry in Kyūshū. After the death of Hideyoshi, **Tokugawa Ieyasu** (1543–1616) founded the dynasty of *shōguns* destined to rule until 1868.

Edo Period (1600–1868)

Tokugawa Ieyasu forced his feudal lords to alternate their time between their own domains and his new capital at Edo (modern-day Tokyo). Japan's long-entrenched code of warrior loyalty now took on the name **Bushidō** (The Way of the Warrior). The samurai, the farmer, the artisan and the merchant became the only socially recognized classes; 'unclean castes', such as tanners and butchers, ossified into the *burakumin* ethnic minority that still exists today.

An uprising by Christians in 1637–38 provoked Iemitsu, the third *shōgun*, to close the country for good in 1639. For the next two centuries, Japan's sole contact with Western science and knowledge was via the Dutch trading post at **Dejima** in Nagasaki.

Castle towns such as Edo, Ōsaka, Nagoya and Kanazawa grew into thriving commercial centres run by merchants. Between fires, earthquakes and other calamities, citizens chose to live for today, not for tomorrow. High levels of literacy encouraged huge demand for printed books; kabuki theatre, and the woodblock prints known as **ukiyo-e** ('floating world pictures') became all the rage.

Western maritime expansion in the first half of the 19th century brought a number of foreign ships to Japanese shores, but only when Commodore Perry arrived in 1853, requesting open access, did Japan's self-imposed isolation begin to crumble. In 1868 an alliance of feudal domains in western Japan successfully brought down the last Tokugawa *shōgun* in the name of the young Emperor Meiji.

Meiji Period (1868–1912)

In 1868 the imperial family moved from Kyoto to Tokyo (Eastern Capital), as Edo was now renamed. Feudalism was gradually dismantled. The **Meiji Constitution** came into effect in1890. Decision-making, however, continued to reside with the ruling oligarchy that had helped to overthrow the Tokugawa *shōgunate*.

Competing factions were able to legitimize their actions in the name of the emperor, a situation which was to have disastrous consequences by the time of World War II.

Meiji Japan also saw the rise of the zaibatsu, indus-trial conglomerates controlled by families such as the

THE CASTLE AND MOMOYAMA ART

Momoyama art is known for its bold, decorative gold-leaf style. It was patronized by war lords like Nobunaga, who commissioned artists of the Kanō school to paint the interior of his splendid castle at Azuchi (long since ruined) on the shores of Lake Biwa. The castle was a great archi-tectural innovation of the late 16th century and the symbol of feudal Japan. The towering **donjon** (castle keep) grew out of samurai-residential and Zen-pavilion architecture, exemplified by Ginkaku-ji and Kinkaku-ji in Kyoto. The castle walls were designed to withstand the fire of cannons, first intro-duced by the Portuguese.

Mitsubishi and Sumitomo. Thirst for foreign knowledge to aid 'Civilization and Enlightenment' reached unparalleled proportions. The tangible benefits of new Western military science came in the **Sino-Japanese** war of 1894–95, when Japan trounced China over the issue of control of Korea.

Above: *School children today still wear uniforms that resemble those worn in the Meiji Period.*
Opposite: *The Atomic Bomb Dome, Hiroshima: a sombre reminder of the past.*

Taishō Period (1912–26)

With World War I came a boom providing munitions to the Allies. Then recession hit, bringing social protest, liberalism, Marxism and even a home-grown version of the Roaring Twenties. In 1923 the music stopped when the Great Kantō Earthquake devastated Tokyo. Worldwide depression followed in 1929, ushering in a decade of fear.

HISTORICAL CALENDAR

ca. AD552 Introduction of Buddhism from Korea.
AD710 Capital established at Nara.
AD794 Capital established at Heian-kyō (Kyoto).
c1010 Murasaki Shikibu writes *The Tale of Genji*.
1185 Beginning of seven centuries of military rule.
1281 Second attempted invasion by the Mongols.
1333 Muromachi *bakufu* established in Kyoto.
1549 Francis Xavier introduces Christianity.
1592 Hideyoshi's first Korean campaign.
1639 Tokugawa Iemitsu closes the country.
1657 Great Meireki Fire kills 100,000 in Tokyo.

1707 Last eruption of Mt Fuji.
1853 Commodore Perry arrives at Uraga Bay.
1868 Power restored to the Meiji Emperor.
1894–95 Japan wins the Sino-Japanese War.
1904–05 Japan wins the Russo-Japanese War, the first Asian victory over a Western power.
1910 Annexation of Korea.
1923 Great Kantō Earthquake.
1937 Rape of Nanjing.
1941 Pearl Harbor bombed.
1945 Atomic bombs dropped on Hiroshima and Nagasaki; Japan surrenders.
1946 New constitution promulgated. Women get the vote.

1952 Allied Occupation ends.
1964 Tokyo hosts Olympics.
1972 Okinawa handed back by the USA.
1989 The death of Emperor Hirohito. His son, Akihito, succeeds.
1995 Great Hanshin-Awaji Earthquake devastates Kōbe.
2001 Koizumi becomes prime minister.
2002 Japan co-hosts FIFA World Cup.
2006 Princess Kiko gives birth to the first male heir to the Crysanthemum throne in 40 years.
2007 Yasuo Fukuda becomes prime minister.
2010 Naoto Kan, co-founder of Japan's Democratic Party, becomes Prime Minister.

Showa Period (1926–89)

With Hitler rampaging across Europe in 1940, East Asian colonies of the Allied forces were at the mercy of the Japanese. After the Japanese bombing of **Pearl Harbor** on 7 December 1941, Hong Kong, Manila, Singapore and Rangoon all fell in rapid succession. Throughout 1942 the Axis Powers (Japan, Germany and Italy) swept across Southeast Asia. Only in 1944 did the USA start to bring the Japanese mainland to its knees, by carpet-bombing virtually all major cities except Kyoto. The end came abruptly with the **atomic bombings** of Hiroshima and Nagasaki in August 1945. Japan surrendered.

Under General Douglas MacArthur, the **Allied Occupation** (1945–52) oversaw the dismantling of the Japanese war machine, including the dissolution of the zaibatsu. The Emperor was allowed to remain as a **constitutional monarch** within a framework of party politics, but **General Tōjō Hideki** and others were sentenced to death at the Tokyo War Crimes Trials.

After June 1950, the **Korean War** triggered a surge in economic growth by boosting Japan's heavy industry. The 1960s, however, proved socially volatile, beginning with bitter protests against the revision of the US-Japan Security Treaty and ending with demonstrations against the Vietnam War that semi-paralyzed university life in Japan.

The **Tokyo Olympics** in 1964 symbolized Japan's return to the world stage.

Inflation rocketed after the oil shock of 1973, but Japan coped and growth resumed. The death of Emperor Hirohito in 1989 marked the end of an era. Under Emperor Akihito, political, social and economic turbulence returned.

The Crysanthemum Throne

Emperor Akihito, the first born son of Emperor Hirohito, acceded to the throne on January 7, 1989. He has overseen a

COLONIZATION

Japan's reward for winning the Sino-Japanese War in 1895 was the island of Formosa (Taiwan). In 1904–05 Japan once again emerged victorious from the **Russo-Japanese** War, gaining territory in Manchuria and Sakhalin. In 1910 it also annexed Korea. After seizing Manchuria in 1931, it went on to set up the puppet state of **Manchukuo** in 1932, the year that also saw the establishment of Unit 731, which was infamous by the end of World War II for its Nazi-style human biological experiments. In the run up to the Pacific War came the invasion of China in 1937 and the **Rape of Nanjing**. China, however, did not give in.

tumultous 20 years both with the country's financial high and lows, and with the inability of his three children to produce a male heir. Princess Kiko, wife of Emperor Akihito's second son, finally provided the country with a male heir in 2006. Crown Prince Hiro married Masako Owada in June 1993, and they have one daughter, Princess Aiko.

GOVERNMENT AND ECONOMY
Constitution

The **Constitution of Japan**, adopted on 3 May 1947, sought to eliminate the ambiguity of the Meiji Constitution by combining a **constitutional monarchy** with a British-style **parliamentary political system**.

The present post-war constitution renounces Japan's sovereign right to war and enshrines the rights of its people, the separation of religion and state and an independent judicial framework resting with a **Supreme Court**. It also designates the emperor as 'the symbol of state and of the unity of the people'. In May 2009 the Japanese judiciary underwent its first changes since World War II, with the number of lawyers, judges and prosecutors rising from around 20,000 to 50,000 (by 2018), and the introduction of a new trial system.

The highest organ of state is the Diet, consisting of the **House of Representatives** (the lower chamber) with 480 members elected to four-year terms, and the **House of Councillors** (the upper chamber) with 252 members elected to six-year terms. Both houses function by committee, much like the American Congress. Executive power resides with the **cabinet**, which is answerable to the Diet. The **prime minister** is appointed by the emperor on the Diet's recommendation.

Below: *The National Diet Building, Kokkaigijidō, seat of Japan's parliament.*

Left: *A typical working farm in Hokkaidō, Japan's dairy heartland.*

Politics and Bureaucracy

The cabinet system started in Japan on 22 December 1885, with the inauguration of the first cabinet led by Hirboumi Ito, the country's first prime minister. Japanese citizens may vote from the age of 20.

The **Liberal Democratic Party** (LDP) ruled Japan from 1955 until 1993, when it was forced into a temporary alliance with the Japan New Party, the Japan Renewal Party and finally the Social Democratic Party of Japan, by an electorate disenchanted with money-power politics. During the 1990s no less than seven prime ministers came and went. From 1996, the LDP was once again in power, although in coalition with various parties. Naoto Kan was elected in June 2010 as Japan's 94th Prime Minister.

What keeps the wheels of state turning is Japan's **civil service**, an elite body of mostly Tokyo University graduates that staff the prime minister's office and 12 ministries. The Bank of Japan, the Ministry of Finance and the Ministry of Economy Trade and Industry rule the country's economy.

Agriculture and Fishing

During the 20th century, **agriculture** dropped from 40% of Gross Domestic Product to just over 2%; only 4.2% of the workforce now farms. The farming sector has been inherently inefficient ever since the Land Reform Act of 1945–46 limited the size of land holdings; the status quo is sustained by a network of **subsidies** and **import controls**, particularly on **rice**. In 1999, government removed the ban on imports of foreign rice, but still imposes heavy protectionist taxes. The government has made moves to lessen its control over the industry, making it more susceptible to market forces, but increasingly

ENERGY

Between 1965–74 Japan's demand for energy grew at an astonishing 10% per annum. Japan still has a greater dependence on imported energy (84%) than any other industrialized nation, but its reliance on crude oil has dropped consistently, from 75% in 1973 to around 50% in 2003. The oil crises of the 1970s led both to greater energy efficiency and diversification of energy sources. By power source, around 56% of electricity is generated by fossil fuels and 32% by nuclear power. Reliance on oil was 49% in 2005. Solar power targets have been met, but is still very small compared to EU countries. On 9 June, 2008, Japanese Prime Minister Yasuo Fukuda said Japan plans to increase the use solar power by ten-fold by 2020, and forty-fold in 2030. To achieve the target, the country aims to have 70 percent of new houses installed with residential photovoltaic systems. Japanese citizens remain understandably ambivalent about the nuclear industry after numerous scares and accidents, notably at Tōkaimura in 1999.

Above: *The Shinkansen (bullet train) pulls out of Kyoto station on the Tōkaidō line between Tokyo and Hakata in Kyūshū.*

has to subsidzse rice farmers who are being hit by falling consumption. The market is now technically open, but imported rice accounts still for only 5.9% of the domestic market (figure from 2008). The World Trade Organization continues to try and whittle away Japan's highly regulated environment both in the agricultural sector and other areas.

Japan is just over 40% self-sufficient in essential foods. Demand for meat and wheat-based foods continues to grow. **Marine products** remain a crucial part of the diet and Japan is the world's biggest importer of fish. It is also one of the few active whaling nations left – much to the disapproval of environmentalists.

Trade and Industry

In 1952 Japan produced just 4800 cars; in 2008 its output was 11.4 million vehicles (but it has been dropping sharply). From the ruins of World War II, Japan emerged as a major economy, second only to the USA in Gross Domestic Product, though China is now an increasingly important trading partner.

Japan's top **exports** include automobiles, semiconductors, electronic components, office equipment and optical instruments. Ships and steel, though still important, come way down the list. Japan has very few natural resources of its own, so its main **imports** inevitably include fossil fuels, food, raw materials and chemicals. By the end of the 20th century the service sector (retail trade, data processing, tourism and entertainment) had become a large and growing component of the economy.

From Trade Friction to Speculative Bubble

By the early 1980s Japan had amassed a huge **trade surplus** with the USA and Europe. At the **Plaza Accord** of 1985, G7 member countries decided to orchestrate a rise in the yen, to make Japan export less and import more. The yen

---

THE VIRTUAL CONGLOMERATE

In 1981, Masayoshi Son, a maverick of Korean heritage, established **Softbank**, a publisher of PC magazines and wholesaler of PC and mobile software. Today he is blazing Japan's trail into the 21st century as one of the biggest investors in the Internet, with huge stakes in household Internet names like *Yahoo!*, as well as in fledgling ventures. Son is probably the only CEO in the world to have a 300-year corporate plan aimed at global Internet domination. Ranked 129 on Forbes' billionaire list in 2007, he is Japan's 5th richest man (despite losing US$70 billion in the 2000 dot-com crash!)

obliged by doubling in value from ¥250 to ¥121 against the US dollar by the end of 1987, which alleviated the trade surplus for a while. To slow the yen's rise, however, the government slashed interest rates, inadvertently paving the way for a **speculative boom** in property, golf club memberships, paintings and fine wines.

On an island awash with cash, the **value of land** began to soar as banks encouraged individuals and businesses to borrow cheaply against the value of increasingly **inflated assets**. By the end of 1989, the Nikkei stock market index had rocketed to an all time high of ¥38,915. The stratosphere – or so it seemed – was the limit.

But by the time the Tokyo Metropolitan Government had moved into its new skyscrapers in Shinjuku in 1992, the Ministry of Finance had instructed banks to cut back their lending. The stock market bubble had already burst. As land prices, too, began to plummet, the Japanese **miracle** turned into a **nightmare**.

From Recession to Recovery and Back Again
In the late 1980s Japan's **banks** were among the largest in the world. In the 1990s, however, financial sector profits collapsed under the weight of bad debts. Notable **bankruptcies** included Yamaichi Securities, Japan's fourth largest stockbroker.

The financial and manufacturing sectors began restructuring in a bid to cut bloated work forces and increase productivity. By the late 1990s unemployment had soared to nearly 5%. For the first time, cardboard cities in parts of Tokyo and elsewhere had become part of the cityscape.

After an era of **deflation** and interest rates close to zero, **growth** has resumed gradually. From Feb 2003 the economy started showing definite signs of recovery. Unemployment peaked at 5.4% in 2002, went to 5.3% in 2003 (its first improvement in 13 years) and as of April 2010 the unemployment rate was 5.1%. Annual

> #### ECONOMIC FACTS AND FIGURES
>
> Japanese Gross National Income (GNI) per capita is around US$36,599, compared with US$41,976 in the USA and US$36,429 in the UK. Over 75% of the population now own a mobile phone (or two or three in the case of teenagers) and over 64.6% of households own personal computers. Tobacco consumption has fallen over the past few years, and the smoking rate fell to 26% of the adult population in 2007 (40.2% of men). They consume around 50 litres of beer per capita annually. Around 65% rank dining out as their top leisure activity, followed by karaoke (44.7%) and then lotteries (with 41.7%).

Below: *All action at the Tokyo Stock Exchange is electronic these days.*

Gross Domestic Product in 2009 grew at 4.6% following government stimulus, and interest rates now stand at 0.1%. 21st-century Japan is no longer a hospitable cradle-to-grave society, yet it remains a formidable economic powerhouse, increasingly fuelled by small, high-tech companies built on meritocracy and American-style incentives. However, the economy continues to be fragile.

Relations with Asia

China and Korea still have a deep-seated antipathy to Japan stemming from war-time issues, but business is the cement that binds the region. Japan has a significant amount of manufacturing capacity in countries such as China and Thailand.

Demographics

The greatest problem presently facing Japan is an **ageing society**. By approximately 2030 nearly 30% of its population will be over 65 compared with 19% in the USA and 21% in the UK. Average life expectancy is now over 78 for men and 85 for women, yet the birth rate is dropping; 1.37 children per woman, far below the 2.1 needed to keep the population steady. Funding the increasing cost of the elderly is already proving a strain on public finances.

THE PEOPLE
Ethnicity

The Japanese are fiercely proud of their ethnic **homogeneity**, while carefully ignoring their virtually indisputable Korean origins. The main indigenous minorities in Japan are three million or so *burakumin* (*see* pages 15 and 94) and around 24,000 **Ainu**. There are also around 607,419 **Koreans** (31% of all foreigners living in Japan), mostly descended from forced labour brought over after 1910, as well as 700,000 Chinese living in Japan. All minorities are forced into the mould of Japanese society; Japanese citizenship, for example, requires having a Japanese name. Ethnic relations still tend to be characterized by discrimination and distrust.

Social Values

For all the turmoil of the 1990s, consensus, conformity and a dislike of confrontation are still deeply embedded in the Japanese psyche. The cement that binds society remains a set of asymmetrical relationships and values inherited from feudal times. ***Giri*** or ***on*** (an obligation, or debt of gratitude) must always be repaid. This partly explains the obsessive levels of gift-giving in Japan, where designer labels and expense count more than the thought.

Education and Work

Japan has a literacy rate of 99%. Over 95% of children complete Senior High School and around one third go on to higher education of some sort. Status is very important in education: the ideal toddler will get into the right kindergarten, on the ladder to a top university and a good job.

Above: *Kanji, the art of calligraphy by brush.*
Opposite: *Bride and groom in traditional dress.*

The intervening period is less appealing: endless hours of supplementary lessons at ***juku*** (crammer schools), the threat of bullying and no longer the promise of a job for life at the end of it. Today, teachers are encouraging greater individuality, but the system is unlikely to change overnight.

Language

Japanese has grammatical similarities to **Korean**. However, it is closer in some respects to the languages of **Austronesia** and the **Pacific Islands**, particularly in vocabulary and syllabic repetition (e.g. *peko-peko* = hungry, *guru-guru* = in circles).

Japanese is quite unlike Chinese. Chinese is monosyllabic, tonal and non-inflecting. Japanese is polysyllabic, non-tonal and inflecting. For an English speaker, pronouncing Japanese is no harder than pronouncing Italian. Syllables are **consonant-vowel** combinations and are evenly stressed, e.g. sake (Japanese rice wine) = sa-ke. The place name Hakone = Ha-ko-ne (not Hak-own or Ha KOH-ne). A macron sign denotes a long vowel, e.g. jū (ten) is pronounced 'joo'.

GLOSSARY OF SUFFIXES

The following suffixes are used throughout this book:
-dake = peak, e.g. Rausu-dake
-dera or -ji = temple, e.g. Sugimoto-dera, Shuzen-ji
-dōri or -dō = street or road, e.g. Nakamachi-dōri, Nakasen-dō
-dō = hall, e.g. Konjiki-dō
-en = garden, e.g. Kenroku-en
-gū, -jingu (or jinja) = shrine, e.g. Tōshō-gū, Asakusa Jinja
-hashi/bashi = bridge, e.g. Nijūbashi
-jō = castle, e.g. Himeji-jō
-kawa/-gawa = river, e.g. Naka-gawa
-ko = lake, e.g. Mashū-ko
-kōen = park, garden
-ryōri = cuisine
-saka or -zaka = slope
-shima or -jima = island
-taki = waterfall
-yama or -san/-zan = mountain, e.g. Taka-yama, Osore-zan

Loan words suffer from the fact that Japanese has no 'v' or 'l' sounds, and often develop a different meaning e.g. 'Baikingu' = Viking = buffet. Loan words are also often truncated, e.g. wāpuro = word processor.

Respect language is highly complex, requiring the altering of verb endings (or the use of different verbs altogether) to indicate **status**.

Above: *Itinerant monk of the Sōtō Zen sect collecting alms. Pilgrims wear hats like this to protect themselves against the sun.* **Opposite:** *The Great Buddha (Daibutsu) of Kamakura is a representative of Amida Buddha, guardian of the Western Paradise.*

Writing

Japanese is written vertically from right to left and horizontally from left to right. Four systems are used together. **Kanji** (Chinese characters) form the backbone of the script; officially there are 1945 recognized *kanji* used for items such as nouns and verbs. One *kanji* may have several different readings. Japanese also uses two phonemically identical but visually distinct syllabaries, **hiragana** and **katakana**, both originating in *kanji*. *Hiragana* is cursive and used to write grammatical elements. *Katakana* looks squarer and is used mainly for non-Chinese foreign words. Japanese also uses the **Roman alphabet** for acronyms such as WTO.

Religion

Religion in Japan is a peculiarly eclectic affair; the stuff of social ritual and superstition, not a philosophical attempt to fathom the meaning of life. It is common for a Japanese child blessed by a Shinto priest to go on to a glitzy Christian-style wedding and depart this world in a Buddhist cremation.

Shinto (**The Way of the Gods**) is a uniquely Japanese blend of animism and ancestor worship. Its aim is to keep the kami (deities) happy through a mixture of purification and ritual. Kami are ubiquitous, mysterious and very powerful; they range from natural spirits lurking on mountains or in trees to departed spirits that preside over distinct skills, like Sugawara Michizane, the kami of learning.

ITEMS SOLD AT SHRINES AND TEMPLES

omikuji: white pieces of paper telling your fortune, drawn by lots. People tend to leave unfavourable *omikuji* twisted round tree branches before leaving a shrine so that they will not come true.
omamori: good luck amulets of all kinds.
ema: pictorial wooden tablets which people inscribe with their wishes for everything from good health to finding a boy- or girlfriend. These too are left hanging in shrine grounds.

The emphasis of Shinto is life: fertility, marriage and other rites of passage, for which Shinto priests perform elaborate **ritual** ceremonies. Blood, dirt and death are all sources of pollution to be avoided. Invoking the kami at a **shrine** requires purifying the hands and mouth with water ladled from a stone basin before tossing a coin or two into the shrine's coffers, clapping the hands twice and offering a prayer.

Shinto thrives on **festivals** called ***matsuri***, which originated as celebrations of the rice-growing cycle and the wellbeing of the whole community. At a *matsuri* the local kami is invited to visit the human world. This entails taking it on a bumpy ride in a portable shrine (*mikoshi*) to present to crowds of festival goers. *Matsuri* involve the beating of drums, dancing, food and, invariably, a hangover.

Japan has 14 **public holidays** (*see* page 126), the most important of which is New Year. Another big event is **Bon** (Festival of Lanterns) in August, when people travel to their ancestral villages to welcome back the departed spirits. The most charming spectacle is **Shichi-go-san** ('Seven-Five-Three') when young children, aged seven, five and three, dress up to visit their local shrines.

Mahayana (Greater Vehicle) Buddhism, or Esoteric Buddhism, arrived from China via Korea ca. AD552. The **Tendai** sect, established in AD805 by the monk Saichō on Hiei-zan near Kyoto, attaches paramount importance to the chanting of the Lotus Sutra. **Shingon** (True Word) Buddhism, founded by Kūkai on Kōya-san (near Ōsaka) is characterized by highly esoteric ritual not dissimilar to Tibetan Buddhism.

As Japan descended into social unrest during the 12th century, pessimism grew that *mappō* (the latter days of the Buddhist Law) had arrived. This resulted in a surge in **Popular Buddhism**, offering quick-fix

CONTEMPORARY THEATRE

Shingeki (new theatre) originated in the Meiji Period as a realistic form of drama influenced by Shakespeare. *Shōgekijō* ('small theatre') or *angura* (from 'underground') developed in the 1960s. Today it focuses on social aspects of Japan's post-war materialism. At the other end of the scale is *Takarazuka*, women's revenge on the all-male world of Kabuki and Nō. *Takarazuka* is an all-female dance and musical chorus with male impersonators; even its fans are women. In 1913 Kobayashi Ichizō founded the first theatre in Takarazuka, near Osaka. There is also one in Tokyo. (Tokyo *Takarazuka* Theatre, 1-1-3 Yurakucho Chiyoda-ku, Tokyo 100-0006)

Below: *In Kyoto,* maiko *(apprentice* geisha*) start training as young as six years old.*

salvation. Pure Land Buddhism taught that invoking the name of **Amida Buddha** would guarantee the soul's entry to the Western Paradise.

Zen Buddhism was introduced from China in the late 12th and early 13th century. Its emphasis on austerity and meditation made it the religion of the samurai. Linked with peaceful gardens, the tea ceremony and the martial arts, it is the most culturally influential school of Japanese Buddhism, particularly associated with Kyoto and Kamakura.

Christianity came to Japan in 1549 with the Jesuit missionary **Francis Xavier**. After periods of vicious persecution it was eventually banned completely in the mid-17th century; whole Christian communities were driven underground for over two centuries. Today, approximately 1% of the Japanese population is Christian.

Traditional Performing Arts

Japan has a rich tradition of **dance** and **music**. Ancient Shinto dances called **kagura**, are still performed today, notably at **Takachiho** in Kyūshū. **Gagaku** is a form of court music that arrived from the Asian continent in the 8th century; when accompanying masked dancing, it is called **bugaku**.

Japan has three traditional forms of **theatre**. **Nō** is a form of classical drama that evolved in the 14th century. Plays fall into five categories: gods, warriors, women, mad women or men, and demons or ghosts. All actors are male and speak in classical language virtually incomprehensible to native Japanese speakers without previous study. The **shite** (principal character) wears a mask and fabulous brocade costume. The Nō stage is bare apart from a pine tree backdrop; the action is slow and elegant.

Kyōgen ('mad words') punctuates a Nō performance in the same way as the Fool in Shakespearean plays. Kyōgen is a colloquial, comic dialogue between two characters, usually a feudal lord and his retainer.

Kabuki is as showy and exuberant as the merchant class of Edo Japan that patronized it. It, too, developed into an all-male theatre form in the 17th century, sustained by

dynasties of actors famous for sequences of proscribed movements ending in a *mie* (climactic pose).

Bunraku (puppet theatre), accompanied by chanting and the shamisen (a stringed instrument), revolves around much the same plots as kabuki (e.g. love tragedies). The puppets, skilfully manipulated by three operators, look like mini-kabuki actors.

Above: *Kimonos, in a wonderful variety of colours, can be purchased in Old Tokyo.*

Arts and Crafts

Japan is a veritable paradise of traditional arts and crafts, ranging from the priceless to perfectly affordable items.

Ceramics include both stoneware and porcelain. In the 16th century, 'The Way of Tea' spurred on the development of tea wares such as **Raku** and **Oribe**. Even today, the most prized tea bowls have a pedigree and even their own name. Many regions have their own rustic pottery traditions including Bizen, Shigaraki and Mashiko. Karatsu in Kyūshū produces stoneware reminiscent of Korean folk pottery. Kyūshū is also the home of Japanese **porcelain** (*see* panel, page 113), which made its debut in the early 17th century.

The Japanese have always prized **lacquer** for its durability. Lacquer production employs a bewildering array of artistic techniques ranging from carving to inlay. Many regions have their own traditions including Wajima (Noto Peninsula) and Kamakura.

As the old feudal order crumbled in the 1870s and

UKIYO-E

Ukiyo-e (wood block prints) became highly popular in the 18th century. The term **ukiyo** (floating world) shed its melancholic Buddhist overtones of 'impermanence' and came to symbolize hedonistic living-for-the-moment. The first *ukiyo-e* grew out of genre painting and appeared as book illustrations. Gradually, however, they became an independent art form covering a huge variety of subjects from **courtesans**, **sumō wrestlers** and pin-up **kabuki actors** to flower and bird subjects, as well as series of landscapes by prolific artists such as Hokusai (1760–1849). Meiji Period prints began to depict new subjects such as railways.

Japanese men abandoned traditional dress for Western 'high collar' fashions, practical items such as sword fittings, *inrō* (medicine cases) and *netsuke* (carved toggles for fastening bags) turned into pieces of decorative art. Metalworkers, ivory carvers and lacquer workers began making **cloisonné** vases, **ivory** figurines and boxes that became the backbone of Meiji export art.

Attractive gifts include **bamboo baskets** and items of *washi* (Japanese paper). Old textiles such as **second hand wedding kimonos** and *obis* (belts) can also be used to good effect as wall hangings. *Tansu* (chests of drawers from the Edo and Meiji periods) make highly attractive, if expensive, pieces of furniture.

Above: *Baseball mania begins at an early age.*

Sports and Recreation

Sumō and baseball are Japan's top two spectator sports. *Sumō* is Shinto in origin, as all the accompanying paraphernalia and ceremony suggest. Pre-match posturing can take several minutes, but the bout itself lasts only a few seconds, ending in one of numerous classified 'throws'. Today's top *sumō* wrestlers are veritable **human bulldozers** weighing on average 156kg (344lb), a hefty 30kg (66lb) more than in the 1970s. Becoming a *yokozuna* (grand champion) is a passport to instant national stardom.

Baseball became a professional sport in Japan in 1934 and has an obsessive following. The Central and Pacific leagues each have six teams. **Soccer**, too, has caught on in a big way since the establishment of the J League in 1992. The FIFA World Cup, co-hosted by Japan and South Korea in 2002, has boosted enthusiasm even further, particularly for England's former captain and star, David Beckham.

To millions of businessmen golf is a ritualistic fusion of business and social life. **Skiing** opportunities are plentiful both in Hokkaidō and the Japan Alps. Ski lifts tend to be crowded on weekends, but a little planning can still mean a good trip. The most popular leisure destination in Japan is Tokyo Disneyland and Disney Sea – attracting 25.82 million people in 2009.

Food and Drink

Restaurants in Japan's big cities serve everything from caviar to curry, but in more remote areas local dishes are still very much the rule. Meat has only been fully part of the Japanese diet since the 19th century.

Kaiseki-ryōri is the Rolls-Royce of traditional cuisine, consisting of endless, exquisitely prepared dishes of fish, vegetables, rice and meat. **Shōjin-ryōri** is Buddhist vegetarian cuisine based on **tōfu** and **sansai** (mountain greens). **Nabe** (stew) is a melange of items thrown in a pot with noodles; a high protein version called **Chanko nabe** is what fuels **sumō** wrestlers.

The ubiquitous **bentō** (lunch box) contains anything from lacquer trays of beautifully prepared rice and vegetables to the take-away *eki-ben* (station lunch box), an often unspeakably disgusting fusion of cold rice and congealed tempura.

The Japanese enjoy drinking. Each year they quaff millions of kilolitres of **beer** and **sake**. Japanese lagers such as Asahi, Kirin and Sapporo are the most popular brews, although Guinness has also arrived big time. **Shōchū**, distilled from rice, barley or potatoes, is like rough vodka, but can be good. Whisky is the drink of bars. Since 1965, wine consumption has more than trebled; some progress has been made in growing Chardonnay and Cabernet Sauvignon grapes in Japan, but France and Australia need not worry about their wine exports yet. The first Japanese wine made from the indigenous Koshu grape was exported to the EU in 2008.

> ### SOME POPULAR DISHES
>
> *donburi* – hot rice with different toppings
> *oden* – stew with fish cake
> *okonomiyaki* – savoury Japanese pancake
> *rāmen* – Chinese-style noodles
> *sashimi* – slices of raw fish
> *shabu-shabu* – thin beef dipped in sesame sauce
> *soba* – thin buckwheat noodles
> *sukiyaki* – thin beef dipped in sweet sauce
> *sushi* – fish on vinegared rice
> *tempura* – battered prawns and vegetables
> *tonkatsu* – deep-fried pork
> *yakitori* – grilled skewers of chicken
> *udon* – fat white noodles
> *unagi* – grilled eel

Below: *A family sits down to dinner in Tokyo.*

2
Tokyo and Kantō

In the 1600s Tokyo was an insignificant fishing village. By the 18th century it had exploded into the world's biggest city, with around 1.3 million inhabitants. Burned to ashes on several occasions, flattened by earthquakes in 1855 and 1923, and carpet-bombed by allied forces in 1945, it has risen time and time again.

Coming in from Narita Airport, the skyline is stupendously ugly, yet it conceals delightful pockets of the old, the new, the conservative, the wacky, the sophisticated and the downright tacky. Tokyo is a triumph of style over substance, because it never quite knows when next it may have to reinvent itself.

It takes just an hour on the circular Yamanote Line to ride from **Old Tokyo**, beneath the cherry blossoms of Ueno and Asakusa, through **Establishment Tokyo**, epitomized by the Imperial Palace and the Ginza, to **Cool Tokyo** in the shops and restaurants of Harajuku and skyscrapers of Shinjuku. **Virtual Tokyo**, the futuristic city out in Tokyo Bay, is an essential side trip.

On the outskirts of the great metropolis, there are several compelling day or weekend excursions, which can easily be made by train: a walk on 'The Bluff' in Yokohama and a meal in Chinatown, or a trip to the temple town of **Kamakura**, the Kyoto of the east, only smaller and more intimate. To the north lies **Nikkō**, home to the grand mausoleum of Tokugawa Ieyasu, the *shōgun* who first made Tokyo his capital. Finally, the **Miura Peninsula** offers some lovely coast to explore and several walking opportunities.

DON'T MISS

★★★ Asakusa: a tantalizing taste of Old Tokyo.
★★★ Tokyo National Museum: Hōryū-ji treasures from the 7th century.
★★★ Meiji Jingū and Harajuku: from Shinto to shopping.
★★★ Shinjuku: from high life to low life.
★★★ Kamakura: the Kyoto of the east.
★★★ Nikkō National Park: exotic Tokugawa mausoleum and Kegon Falls.
★★ Yokohama: Minato Mirai 21, Chinatown and 'The Bluff'.

Opposite: *Paying homage to the Great Buddha of Kamakura.*

OLD TOKYO

In atmosphere, **Asakusa** firmly belongs to the *shitamachi* (low city/downtown) of old Edo, where merchants and artisans lived in the equivalent of London's East End. The samurai inhabited the *yamanote* (high city/uptown) to the west, but down in the pleasure quarters of Yoshiwara, samurai and merchant alike enjoyed an exotic demi-monde of theatrical and sexual entertainment offered by courtesans.

By the 1920s, Asakusa had become a lively theatre, cinema and cabaret district. Just outside the Yamanote Loop, this is a good starting point for a journey through the low and high life of Tokyo, and can be reached by boat up the Sumida River from Hinode Pier near Hamamatsu-chō. The World Trade Centre provides a good night view of Tokyo.

Ueno Park is Tokyo's largest natural playground. North of Ueno, near Nishi-Nippori, the **Yanaka** cemetery area affords another glimpse of old Tokyo with temples and traditional wooden houses. Yanaka is also the burial place of the last Tokugawa *shōgun*. Tokyo's consumer electronics Mecca, **Akihabara**, lies to the south.

Senō-ji
(Asakusa Kannon) ★★★

Asakusa's **Kaminari-mon** (Thunder Gate) sports an enormous red lantern. It is also guarded on either side by the gods of wind and rain, posing like two kabuki actors. Beyond

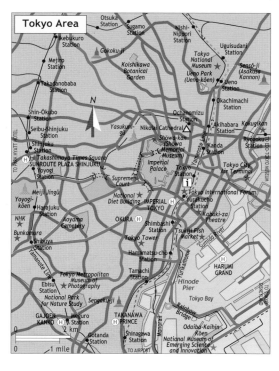

lies **Nakamise-dōri**, an alleyway packed with shops selling *sembei* (rice crackers), toys, dolls, traditional combs, umbrellas and paper wallets. There is a festive atmosphere here any day of the year, but Asakusa also hosts more than its fair share of Tokyo's festivals.

Ahead, beyond the two-storeyed treasure gate, is the **main hall** of **Asakusa Kannon**, as the temple is popularly known. According to tradition it was founded in AD628 to house a tiny gold statue of **Kannon** (the goddess of mercy) caught in the nets of two fishermen. The present building dates only from 1958, though it is hard to tell. In front, high-heeled teenagers and wizened elderly people alike stop at an imposing bronze censer to purify themselves by wafting fragrant plumes of incense over their heads.

Other landmarks include the 17th-century **Asakusa Jinja** (Shrine) on the right, dedicated to the two Kannon fishermen, and on the left, the reconstructed **pagoda**, which belongs to the **Dembō-in** (Abbot's Residence). The garden is not open to the public.

Ueno Park ★★

Tokyo's first public park, opened in 1873, Ueno Park encompasses the rather charmingly weed-filled Shinobazu Pond and teems with museums and shrines, notably the 17th-century **Ueno Tōshō-gū** (Shrine) which is dedicated to Ieyasu, the first Tokugawa *shōgun*. Though rather dilapidated now, the shrine has a certain old-Edo charm.

Above: *The Rainbow Bridge links Establishment Tokyo with Virtual Tokyo.*

ASAKUSA FESTIVALS

• 18 March and 18 October – **Golden Dragon Dance**.
• Third weekend in May – **Sanja Matsuri**, Tokyo's biggest festival focused on Asakusa Jinja. A riotous procession of *mikoshi* (portable shrines).
• Late July to early August – **Sumida River Fireworks**.
• Late August – **Asakusa Carnival (Samba Festival)**.
• 3 November – **Tokyo Jidai Matsuri**. Re-enactment of a number of historical scenes.
• December – **Hagoita-ichi** (Battledore Fair). Stalls sell elaborately decorated battledores (rackets). *Check with the Asakusa Information Centre situated opposite the Kaminari-mon for full details.*

UENO PARK MUSEUMS

Ancient Orient Museum:
small, private museum with
artefacts from across Asia.
Open 10:00–17:00 Tue–Sun.
**National Museum of
Western Art:** major works
from around the world.
Open 09:30–17:30, Tuesday–
Sunday; Friday evenings until
20:00. Admission fee ¥420.
www.nmwa.go.jp/en
National Science Museum:
from astronomy to natural
history. Somewhat dry.
Open 09:00–17:00, Tuesday–
Sunday; Friday evenings until
20:00. Admission fee ¥600
www.kahaku.go.jp/english
Shitamachi **Museum:** more
reconstructions of life in Edo.
Artisans at work.
Open 09:30–16:30, Tuesday–
Sunday. Admission fee ¥300.

Below: *Purification with
incense before visiting a
temple is a well-established
ritual in Japan.*

Ueno Park also has a **zoo** and a wonderful display of cherry blossoms, which attracts millions of revellers in late March and early April.

Ueno has a *shitamachi* ethos, flanked by prestigious **Tokyo University** to the west, and bars, *rakugo* (comic monologue) theatres, traditional shops and 'soaplands' to the south. **Ameyoko-chō** (Candy Sellers' Alley) by Ueno Station's Shinobazu exit is a melée of stalls selling everything from fresh fish to cheap sports shoes. It started as a black market after the war and it still looks like one.

Tokyo National Museum ★★★

Until the addition of two new wings in 1999, the Tokyo National Museum got full marks for content, but low scores on presentation. Now, Japan's top art collection is infinitely more digestible. The jewel in the crown is the new **Hōryū-ji Hōmotsukan** (Gallery of Hōryūji Treasures), with its rotating display of 7th-century bronze gilt statues, textiles and metalwork from the great temple of Hōryū-ji near Nara. If you have limited time, make this gallery alone your priority.

Of the other buildings, the **Honkan** (main building) houses the permanent collection of Japanese arts; the **Tōyōkan** displays Asian art and antiquities and the **Hyōkeikan** has occasional special exhibitions. The new **Heiseikan** has a permanent Japanese archaeological gallery on the first floor and special exhibitions on the second floor. Open 09:30–17:00 Tue–Sun; Fri until 20:00, Sat and Sun until 18:00. Admission ¥600.

Edo-Tokyo Museum ★★

To make the transition from Edo to Tokyo, it is worth heading east across the Sumida River from Akihabara to Ryōgoku. Ryōgoku is home not only to the **Kokugikan**, Tokyo's National *Sumō* Stadium, but also to the **Edo-Tokyo Museum**, which uses a high-tech environment to trace Tokyo's evolution over 400 years.

The museum exterior is an eyesore, but the interior is well-labelled in English, with life-

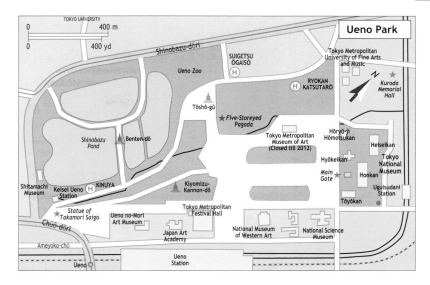

size replicas and audiovisual displays on topics ranging from samurai life to the bombing of Tokyo. This is a vast museum, which should not be rushed. One ticket is valid for re-entry all day. Open 09:30–17:30. Admission ¥450. For more information visit www.edo-tokyo-museum.or.jp

ESTABLISHMENT TOKYO

Old Tokyo and Establishment Tokyo meet in the scholar and bookworm's paradise of **Kanda**, south of Akihabara. One oddity, near Ochanomizu subway station, is the **Nikolai Cathedral**. Completed by Josiah Conder in 1891, it is named after the Russian priest, Nikolai, who first spent three years in Hakodate before arriving in Tokyo in 1872.

Nothing could be more establishment than the grim steel *torii* (gate) of the **Yasukuni Shrine** (*see* www.yasukuni.or.jp/english/index.html). Each year on 15 August controversy rages when ministers turn up to pay their respects to Japan's war dead. Nearby on Yasukuni dōri, the new **Showa-kan** museum dedicated to Emperor Hirohito has also attracted criticism for its anodyne rather than analytical portrayal of the war. Open 09:00–17:30.

Right: *Nijūbashi in the Imperial Palace grounds is a tranquil spot in frantic Tokyo.*

GHIBLI MUSEUM

The *manga* museum, dedicated to films from the Ghibli studio, has rapidly become one of Tokyo's coolest and most popular attractions since it opened a few years ago. Tickets need to be purchased in advance. Open 10:00–18:00, Wednesday–Monday. Inokashira Park, 1-1-83 Simorenjaku, Mitaka-shi. *See* www.ghibli-museum.jp/en

NEW AND NOTABLE

Tokyo's skyline is continually changing. These recent additions will no doubt soon be overtaken by something else, but for now, they are attracting the crowds:
National Art Centre, in Roppongi – 2007, www.nact.jp/english/index.html
Omotesando Hills – 2005, www.omotesandohills.com/english
Roppongi Hills – 2003, www.roppongihills.com/en
Tokyo Sky Tree in Sumida Ward – completion 2011, Herzog & de Meuron's **Prada Building**, Omotesando – 2003, www.prada.com

Tokyo Station is one of the very few Meiji Period buildings that survived the 1923 earthquake. To the west, it deposits its myriad passengers in the **Marunouchi** business district facing the Imperial Palace park. To the east, the crowds pour out into **Nihombashi** and **Kyōbashi**, home to venerable institutions such as the Bank of Japan, Mitsukoshi department store and the **Bridgestone Museum of Art**, a major Western art collection. The maze of malls and passages beneath the station is highly conducive to getting lost. *See* www.bridgestone-museum.gr.jp/en

Towards Yūrakuchō station, Rafael Vinoly's cavernous **Tokyo International Forum** (TIF) is worth visiting for its parabolic glass- and steel-built conference-hall architecture. It also often houses excellent art exhibitions, antique fairs and even flea markets. *See* www.t-i-forum.co.jp/english The collection of Japanese, Chinese and Western antiquities at the **Idemitsu Museum of Art** in the Teikoku Geki-jō building is displayed only a portion at a time. Open 10:00–17:00, Tue–Sun; www.idemitsu.co.jp

Imperial Palace ★

In 1868 the last Tokugawa *shōgun* vacated Tokyo's prime piece of real estate to make way for the imperial family. The inner grounds are open to the public only on 2 January and the Emperor's birthday (23 December), but **Kokyo Gaien** (the palace garden, open to the public) offers a pleasant stroll. The view of Nijūbashi is particularly picturesque. Southwest of the **Imperial Palace** lies the **National Diet**, a dreary wedding-cake structure where Japan's political power presides.

Ginza ★★

After a fire in 1872, Ginza was rebuilt in red brick to symbolize the Meiji ideal of 'Civilization and Enlightenment'; the brick, unfortunately collapsed in the earthquake of 1923.

From **Ginza Yon-chome** crossing, flanked by **Wakō** department store and **Le Café Doutor**, Chūō-dōri has the right sort of stature for the Champs Elysées but is a dowager duchess at heart, sporting Tiffany's, just like Fifth Avenue. Behind the formal façades, however, are many smaller shops and galleries.

Down Harumi-dōri is the unmistakable visage of the **Kabuki-za Theatre**. Opened on this spot in 1889, the new theatre marked the transition of Kabuki from the Low City to the High City: respectability had arrived. Kabuki still draws the crowds and is well worth a visit, even if only to see one act. English tapes can be hired to help follow the plot.

Cool Tokyo

Whatever your age, you will feel like last century's vintage around the legions of chic Japanese setting Tokyo's fashion and lifestyle trends. The young get off the Yamanote Line at **Harajuku** to cut their teeth on the cute and the trendy before graduating to the bars, boutiques and love hotels of **Shibuya**. **Shinjuku** can derail anyone at any age.

Meiji Jingū and Harajuku ★★★

If you have only one hour for a stroll, go to the **Meiji Jingū** opposite Tange Kenzō's 1964 Olympic Stadium. On New Year's Day the shrine is impossibly crowded, but on weekdays the shady, tree-lined avenues are a good escape. The **Inner Garden** is particularly beautiful in June when the **irises** are in bloom. *See* www.meijijingu.or.jp/english/index.html

It is always worth hanging about for a while to see one of the many traditional **marriage ceremonies** held at the shrine. The sight

---

TSUKIJI FISH MARKET

No stay in Tokyo is complete without an obligatory dawn visit to Tsukiji Fish Market a few minutes from Ginza. As the largest fish market in the world, Tsukiji sells over 2.3 million kg (5 million lb) of fish, equivalent to over US$20 million, every day. The number of visitors to the tuna auction from 05:30 is restricted to 140 per day. Visitors are prohibited from entering the market's wholesale area before 09:00. Closed on Sundays and public holidays. The planned move in 2012 is on hold due to pollution worries in the new location. *See* www.tsukiji-market.or.jp/tukiji_e.htm

Below: *The dazzling lights of Ginza Yon-chome crossing by night.*

VIRTUAL TOKYO

A major legacy of the bubble era is the space-pod city still taking shape out in Tokyo Bay. In the early 1990s, when recession hit, the man-made island of Odaiba looked like becoming a veritable Never Never Land. However, it is well worth buying a one-day ticket for the unmanned Yurikamome monorail from Shimbashi for a ride into the future, past the **Tokyo Big Site** (International Exhibition Centre), the **Fuji TV Building**, and on to **Palette Town** housing a MegaWeb Funfair, a history garage of vintage cars and **VenusFort** (see page 40).

Below: *Shinto priests and miko (shrine maidens) still wear Heian Period costume.*

of bride and groom being led across the courtyard by a wand-waving Shinto priest is a flashback to Japan's courtly traditions. Other colourful spectacles include **Coming-of-Age Day** (second Monday of January) and **Shichi-go-san** (15 November).

The approach road to the shrine is **Omote Sandō**. It remains a firm *gaijin* (foreigner) favourite for its range of shops from Issey Miyake to Gap and the Oriental Bazaar. Maranouchi district is increasingly worth visiting for interesting small boutiques. Takeshita-dōri, between Harajuku Station and Meiji-dōri, is where the teenagers hang out; grown-ups may prefer to visit the small **Ōta Memorial Art Museum** that specializes in *ukiyo-e*. *See* www.ukiyoe-ota-muse.jp/index-E.html

Shibuya ★★

After dark the action shifts to the bars, restaurants and cinemas of **Shibuya**, also home to the NHK Broadcasting Centre and the Orchard Hall (part of the wider cultural centre of Bunkamura) for pop, classical music and other entertainment (*see* www.bunkamura.co.jp/english). In the same complex is avant-garde theatre, an arts cinema, a museum, a gallery, and plenty of shops and restaurants. Time has moved on in a big way since the 1920s, when **Hachikō**, the faithful dog depicted in the statue at the west exit of Shibuya station, sat waiting for nine years for his dead master to get off the train and come home.

The redevelopment of the old Sapporo Brewery site at **Ebisu Garden Place**, one stop south of Shibuya, has created an extension of Cool Tokyo (*see* http://gardenplace.jp/english). Situated here is the excellent **Tokyo Metropolitan Museum of Photography** and the free **Yebisu Beer Museum**, open 10:00–18:00, Tuesday–Sunday. The Garden Place Tower has good views and restaurants.

Left: *The futuristic globe of the Fuji TV Building looks out over Tokyo Bay.*

Shinjuku ★★★

Shinjuku is neon-induced schizophrenia incarnate. Choose the west exit of the station that processes a mind-boggling two million people every day and you will find the high life in **Nishi-Shinjuku**, a serene **skyscraper city**. Choose east and you will arrive at the low life of **Kabukichō**, heaving with sex and sleaze – although in a serious attempt to clean up the sleaze there are now cinemas, restaurants, nightclubs as well as the 16th-century shrine Hanazono Jinja. Choose south and you will find the middle road to consumer heaven at **Takashimaya Times Square**, which has an IMAX theatre and Joypolis, a Sega game centre.

Located in Nishi-Shinjuku, the **Tokyo Metropolitan Government Office** complex has observation decks on the 45th floors of both the north and south towers. Open 09:30–17:30, Tue–Fri; 09:30–19:30, Sat, Sun and public holidays. Not far away is the **Tokyo City Opera complex**, which houses the impressive **City Concert Hall** and **New National Theatre**. *See* www.operacity.jp/en Open 11:00–19:00, Tue–Thu and Sun; 11:00–20:00, Fri and Sat.

When it all becomes too much, simply retire to the gardens of **Shinjuku Gyōen** and collapse.

SHOPPING

Tokyo is one gigantic shopping mall. Prices began to come down in the 1990s and there are now thousands of convenience stores, discount stores and even ¥100 stores. Even so, no visitor in their right mind goes to Japan with the purpose of buying a Gucci handbag.

TANGE KENZŌ (1913–2005)

Shinjuku's **Tokyo Metropolitan Government** office complex, completed in 1992, was designed by the prolific architect Tange Kenzō. Tange was first noticed as the winner of a 1942 competition seeking designs for memorials to the Greater East Asia Co-prosperity Sphere. The memorials were never built, but Tange went on to design the **Hiroshima Peace Memorial Museum complex** (completed in 1959), and the **Olympic Stadium** (1964). In 1960 he proposed a grand urban plan for Tokyo Bay that never got off the ground. He did, however, stamp his mark there eventually with the futuristic **Fuji TV building**, opened in 1997.

Above: *Shoppers stroll down Nakamise-dōri mall.*

VENDING MACHINES

As if Japan did not have enough shops, it also has literally millions of vending machines lurking on street corners, in temple grounds and office buildings. The most common items on sale are **cigarettes** and dozens of **designer drinks** ranging from sparkling water to hot and cold tea and coffee. Machines selling beer and whisky have virtually been phased out. In big cities you can also buy anything from batteries to flowers, hot meals, porn videos and disposable cameras. Business hotels often have machines selling **toothbrushes**, **disposable underwear** and **shaving kits**. You can even buy bunches of flowers in vending machines. Language is no barrier and the machines invariably work.

Department stores are cradle-to-grave institutions encompassing art galleries, restaurants, food halls, designer gear, wedding and even funeral services. **Mitsukoshi** in Nihombashi and **Isetan** in Shinjuku (which has a Foreign Customer Service Centre) are two worthy examples of the genre. **Food halls** in department stores make for some of the best shopping – the one in the basement of Matsuzakaya department store, in Ginza, is one of the best.

For the extraordinary spectacle of a Virtual Italy in Japan, go to **VenusFort** at Palette Town in Tokyo Bay. Here, in a fake palazzo setting where the computer-controlled, sky-painted ceiling changes from dawn to dusk every hour, Japanese women shop till they drop in their very own designer boutique theme park. In 2009, VenusFort top floor added the first outlet mall in downtown Tokyo.

Akihabara is the **consumer electronics** capital of Tokyo. All kinds of products, from the first colour television sets to the first DVD players, have made their consumer debut here since the war. Stores also carry various export models. **Nishi-Shinjuku** is famous for **cameras**. **Kanda** is the home of second-hand **bookshops**. **Kappabashi** (near Asakusa) is the centre for kitchen equipment, everyday crockery and the plastic-food models that appear in many restaurant windows.

There are, however, still many traditional arts and crafts shops to be found in Ginza, Nihombashi and Asakusa. The **Japan Traditional Craft Centre** in Ikebukuro has a whole range of items. Flea markets are fun for picking up ceramics and old kimonos.

NIGHTLIFE

From the most exclusive **Ginza Club** to the **Irish Pub**, via the **Nō-pan Kissaten** (No Panty Coffee Shop), where the waitresses wear little more than an apron, Tokyo's nightlife is one long adult version of Alice in Wonderland. Drink is what lubricates the wheels of business in Japan – never mind pleasure – and money will buy anything: the spirit of Yoshiwara is alive and well.

The most respected businessman will be forgiven virtually anything when drunk, but no one is forgiven for failing to pay the bill. Many bars and clubs will not accept credit cards and have a hefty cover charge. The damage to both health and wealth can be immense, so find out what you are paying for before you start.

The traditional hangout for *gaijin* (foreigners) has been **Roppongi**, ever since the Americans adopted it during the Allied Occupation. Crammed with expensive bars, restaurants and clubs, Roppongi is a prime Tokyo nightlife ghetto for those in search of sex, sin and alcohol in varying quantities. Recently, the more upscale Roppongi Hills has typified the newer, more sophisticated crowd in this former nightlife ghetto. Nearby, the Midtown district is also worth exploring for upscale shops and restaurants.

In **Ginza** and **Akasaka** politicians arrive in fleets of sleek, black limousines for a discreet evening's entertainment by a *geisha*, while the young, mobile-phone brigade hang out in **Shibuya**. At the end of a long night, however, **Shinjuku** wins hands down for sheer sleaze. **Kabukichō** is the heart of all things naughty and **Shinjuku Ni-chome** is the heart of **Gay Tokyo**, where *gaijin* must tread rather carefully to gain any acceptance among the local crowd.

KARAOKE

To the Japanese, karaoke ('empty orchestra') is an art form. There are even books and magazines on '**The Way of Karaoke**'. Unsuspecting foreigners cornered in a bar may cringe at the idea of being expected to belt out a Beatles song to a taped soundtrack, but the Japanese take a dim view if you refuse to perform. Drinking copious amounts of sake will help you to get over the embarrassment. Karaoke has grown into a massive industry since its humble origins in the 1970s; it is also one of the few forms of Japanese popular culture to have caught on in the West.

YOKOHAMA

Yokohama is one of Japan's original **treaty ports** opened up in 1858. As such, it is used to hosting foreigners. Despite its status as Japan's second largest city, it is much easier on the eye and more relaxed than Tokyo. The past and future merge spectacularly from the Bluff,

Tokyo and Kantō

Below: *A bustling foreign corner of Japan lies in Yokohama's Chinatown.*

where the moss-covered graves of the **Foreigners' Cemetery** give way to the 21st-century skyline. The World Cup soccer final was held at the Yokohama International Stadium in June 2002.

Minato Mirai 21 (MM 21) ★★

Yokohama's answer to Tokyo Bay is MM21, an ever-evolving world of shopping malls and restaurants. At its heart is the 296m (971ft) **Landmark Tower**, **Queen's Square** and the attractive Meiji-style **Aka Renga Sōko** (Red Brick Warehouses) by Osanbashi Pier, which offer cultural events, bars, live music clubs and yet more shopping. On crystal clear days (all too few) it is worth paying for the fastest lift ride in the world up the Tower to have a look at Mount Fuji in the distance. The **Yokohama Maritime Museum** is marked by the Nippon-Maru docked outside. *See* www.minatomirai21.com/eng

Chinatown ★★

Chinatown grew around the merchants who started trading in Yokohama in the 1870s. At its heart is the gaudy temple of **Guan Yu** (the god of war), which is also the focus of **Chinese New Year** celebrations and the Guan Yu festival in summer. The smoky aroma of roasting ducks and steaming dumplings that wafts up from Chinatown's two hundred or so restaurants is pure Hong Kong. **Ishikawachō** is the closest JR (Japanese Railway) station for Chinatown, Yamate and Motomachi.

Yamate (The Bluff) ★★

Up the hill from boutique-laden **Motomachi** is a series of small lanes leading steeply up to Yamate, the area first inhabited by foreign diplomats, architects and engineers. A series of English information boards with area maps for Yamate, Negishi and Honmoku wards make it easy to have a pleasant stroll around this large area of Yokohama. The nightlife in Yokohama centres around the areas of Ishikawacho and Motomachi.

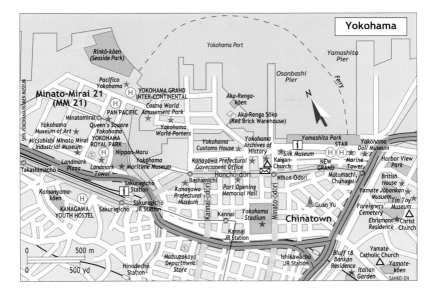

Yokohama

Several historic, wooden houses have been preserved in Yamate: admission is free to the **Erhismann Residence**, the **Bluff 18 Bankan Residence** in the Yamate Italian Garden, the **Diplomat's House** and the **234 Bankan**. By the **Foreigners' Cemetery** is the distinctive, turreted **Yamate Jūbankan**, now a French restaurant with a relaxed tea house on the ground floor.

Sankei-en ★★

Opened to the public by a wealthy silk merchant in 1906, this beautiful garden in Honmoku preserves building styles from all over Japan including a traditional farmhouse, villas and a tea house. The Inner Garden offers the best display. Open daily, 09:00–17:00; tea house open, 10:00–15:30.

KAMAKURA

The warrior **Minamoto Yoritomo** chose this hilly, seaside town as his capital in 1192. Kamakura has a medieval heritage of 65 temples, 19 shrines and a host

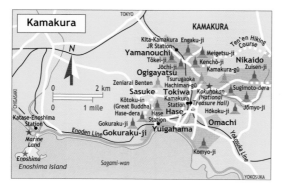

of festivals. In spring, the cherry blossoms are spectacular; in summer, surfers come flocking to what makes a poor alternative to Hawaii. It makes sense to hire a bicycle by the station or just explore on foot. **Komachi-dōri**, parallel with Wakayama Ōji, is fun for its stalls and shops.

Opposite: *The imposing Tsurugaoka Hachiman Shrine was moved to its present site in the heart of Kamakura in 1191.*

Kita (North) Kamakura ★★

Kamakura has **five major Zen temples** characterized by a triple-bay gate (*san-mon*) and buildings aligned on a north-south axis. Kenchō-ji, Engaku-ji, Jūfuku-ji, Jōchi-ji, and Jōmyō-ji all lie in the hills around Kita Kamakura, one stop before Kamakura Station.

A walk around the spacious, cedar-shaded grounds of **Engaku-ji** (open 08:00–17:00, April–October and 08:30–16:00, November–March) is a good antidote to Tokyo fatigue. Nearby is **Tōkei-ji** (open 08:30–17:00, April–October and 08:30–16:00, November–March), a pretty haven where, in the days of the *shōgun*s, abused wives could escape their husbands by becoming nuns.

Linking part of this area is the **Ten'en Hiking Course**, a 90-minute trail that loops north from Zuisen-ji (famous for its plum blossom in February) in the east to **Kenchō-ji** (open 08:30–16:30, year round) in the west, passing *yagura* (burial caves) in the cliffs. It is a further 2km (1.2 miles) from here to Kamakura's main sites. It does get quite steep in parts.

Zeniarai Benten (Money-washing Shrine) ★★★

Zeniarai Benten is Kamakura's quirkiest shrine. Here, at a spring deep within in a cave reached through a succession of *torii* and tunnels, the Japanese religiously wash their money in the hope that **Benten (goddess of fortune)** will double its value. Open year round.

Great Buddha of Kōtoku-in ★★★

The Great Buddha (**Daibutsu**) is Kamakura's most venerable resident. Cast in 1252, he is a gargantuan 11.5m (38ft) hollow, bronze representation of **Amida Buddha**, who guides believers in Pure Land Buddhism to the Western Paradise. Since 1495, when the roof over his head was last destroyed, he has sat al fresco, calmly surviving all disasters known to man.

The temple is open 07:00–18:00, Buddha itself open 08:00–16:30 every day.

Hase-dera ★★

Hase-dera has good views across Sagami Bay. It is also home to the 9m (30ft) **Eleven-headed Kamakura Kannon** (**goddess of mercy**), reputedly Japan's tallest wooden sculpture, dating from the 8th century. Its most poignant inhabitants, however, are hundreds of small stone statues depicting **Jizō** (saviour of children). Dressed in bibs and woolly hats (real baby clothes), they commemorate babies who died before being born.

Tsurugaoka Hachiman-gū (Hachiman Shrine) ★★★

This imposing Minamoto clan shrine is dedicated to **Hachiman** (**god of war**). In spring and autumn it is the venue of major festivals commemorating Kamakura's rich and often bloodstained warrior past. It is also a favourite blossom-viewing spot.

Kokuhōkan (National Treasure Hall) ★★

The National Treasure Hall (east of the Hachiman Shrine) has a rotating display of art, including realistic Kamakura Period statues of Buddhist priests. English labelling is scanty, but the sculptures speak for themselves. **Eastern Kamakura** has a series of small temples off the beaten track. **Sugimoto-dera** is the oldest temple in Kamakura, founded in AD734. Perched

KAMAKURA-BORI

Kamakura is famous for a particular style of **carved lacquerware** known as Kamakura-bori. Black and vermilion carved Chinese lacquer was very popular in 15–16th-century Japan. However, the technique of carving through numerous layers of lacquer was expensive and time consuming. The Japanese decided on a shortcut by carving the wooden base of the object first and then applying the lacquer. Many shops sell Kamakura-bori trays and bowls, some of which cost a small fortune.

Below: *Colourful paper cranes are considered a symbol of longevity.*

at the top of a steep flight of steps, it has a pleasantly chaotic interior, full of chains of paper cranes and dimly lit statues. **Hōkoku-ji** is justly renowned for its bamboo grove, which evokes the atmosphere of Kurosawa's film, *Rashōmon*. Open Tue–Sun 09:00–16:00.

DAY EXCURSIONS

Beyond Kamakura and Yokosuka, the **Miura Peninsula** has some lovely coastal scenery and crashing waves, a bit like Cornwall or Maine. The easiest way to get there is by JR from Shinagawa to Misakiguchi. From here you can also take a bus to the small island of **Jōgashima** and go for a stroll.

The Kantō region has its own mini mountain range only an hour west of Shinjuku on the JR Chūō line. At 600m (1969ft) **Takao-san** is the easiest one-day hike, with several well-signposted routes to the summit. (There is also a cable car.) A longer hiking trail goes on to **Jimba-san**, Takao-san's higher neighbour at 857m (2812ft). The area is busy at weekends, but it is not that hard to get off the beaten track.

About two hours northwest of Tokyo from Ikebukuro station is **Chichibu-Tama National Park**, a favourite spot for autumn colours and home to 20 peaks of over 1980m (6496ft). Again, there are many hiking trails.

Southeast of Nikkō is the pottery village of **Mashiko**, famous for its rustic earthenwares. In 1920 the Japanese potter, Hamada Shōji, went to England to work with Bernard Leach (1887–1979). When he returned to Japan in 1924, he settled in Mashiko and became a leader of the **Mingei** (folk craft) movement, producing work influenced by Korean and Okinawan ceramics. The **Tōgei Messe Mashiko** pottery complex (also woodblock prints and art exhibitions) is open 09:30–16:00, Thursday–Tuesday, November–March (until 17:00, April–October). Good shop next door for buying pottery. Admission fee, ¥600.

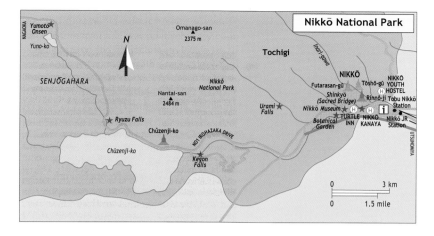

Nikkō National Park ★★★

It took an army of artisans over 20 years to build the Tōshō-gū, the grandiose mausoleum complex of Tokugawa Ieyasu. Completed in 1636, it is Japan's most elaborate piece of chinoiserie. In May and October festivals are held re-enacting the heyday of the **shōguns**.

From a striking five-storeyed pagoda, the route to the mausoleum leads through the Nio-mon, a gate flanked by Buddhist guardians. Next come the Sacred Stables, carved with a famous image of **three monkeys** representing the three principles of Tendai Buddhism (hear no evil, see no evil, speak no evil).

Beyond is the most impressive structure of all: the **Yōmei-mon**, a Baroque structure of vermilion and gilded layers. Other buildings worth seeing are the **Honji-dō**, with its image of a 'crying dragon' on the ceiling, and the connecting **Haiden** (Prayer Hall) and **Honden** (Main Hall). Ieyasu's actual tomb is up a long flight of stone steps, where there is usually some peace and quiet.

Lake Chūzenji, beneath Mount Nantai, lies 10km (6 miles) west of Nikkō up a spectacular series of hairpin bends. It has charming cherry blossoms and autumn colours, but its most spectacular sight is the 97m (318ft) **Kegon Falls**, which freezes in winter.

Tokyo and Kantō at a Glance

Spring offers comfortable temperatures and cherry blossoms. Autumn too is pleasant. Avoid Nikkō on weekends or public holidays (unless you are going specifically for the May or October festivals) or book well ahead. **Winter** can be a very attractive time for sightseeing, with cold, clear days.

GETTING THERE

Narita International Airport is 70km (44 miles) from Tokyo. The **Airport Limousine Bus** service to The Tokyo City Air Terminal (TCAT), and other drop-off points, is the most convenient way into central Tokyo. The **JR Narita Express** (N'EX) to Tokyo Station and Yokohama Station is fast, but expensive. The **Keisei Skyliner** rail service to Ueno is the cheapest. Taking a taxi will leave you bankrupt. Domestic flights arrive at **Haneda Airport**, 20 minutes from Hamamatsu-chō by monorail.

GETTING AROUND

Tokyo's 12 **subway** lines are colour-coded and have English signs. Runs from 05:00–24:00/01:00. Rush hour is around 08:00 and 18:00. Tōei and Eidan lines require separate or transfer tickets. JR lines require separate tickets altogether. Pre-paid cards and carnets (*kaisūken*) are available. Women-only carriages have been introduced. **Taxis** are useful, but fares mount up quickly in traffic. Have your destination written down (in Japanese) to show the driver, who is very unlikely to speak English. In addition, many addresses can be fiendishly difficult to find without a precise map. Doors are open and shut automatically by the driver. Do not interfere! For day excursions to **Yokohama** and **Kamakura** take JR from Tokyo Station. All major Yokohama stations have tourist information centres (the Shinkansen stops at Shin-Yokohama Stn). From Kamakura station the Enoden line is a picturesque route to Hase-dera and on to the island of Enoshima. Bikes for hire at a shop next to Kamakura Station. For **Nikkō** take either the Tōbū-Nikkō line from Asakusa Station, JR from Tokyo or Ueno via Utsunomiya (about two hours). Buy a Nikkō Mini Free Pass from Tōbu Railway (valid for two days) if appropriate. For hiking maps check with the **tourist information centre** between the station and Tōshō-gū (about 15 minutes walk). **Mashiko** is an hour by bus from Utsunomiya.

WHERE TO STAY

LUXURY
Park Hyatt Hotel, 3-7-1-2 Nishi-Shinjuku, Shinjuku-ku, tel: 03 5322 1234. Skyscraper in Tokyo. Home to the excellent **New York Grill** bar and restaurant, tel: 03 5323 3458.
Ritz Carlton Tokyo, Tokyo Midtown, 9-7-1, Akasaka, Minato-ku, tel: 03 3423 8000, www.ritzcarlton.com/en/Properties/Tokyo/Default.htm

In the chic part of Roppongi. For those who can afford it, ultimate pampering and luxury awaits; 248 guest rooms, and a 2000 sq ft spa.

MID-RANGE
Mitsui Urban, 8-6-15 Ginza, Chūō-ku, tel: 03 3572 4131. Good price for location, right by the gleaming stores of Ginza but also easy access to Shinbashi and Hibiya. Primarily a business hotel but clean and friendly.
Claska, 1-3-18 Chuo-cho, Meguro-ko, tel: 03 3719 8121, www.claska.com Boutique-style hotel that has affordably, quirky and rather lovely rooms. Good restaurant and bar also.
Hotel Sunroute Plaza Shinjuku, 151-0053 2-3-1 Yoyogi, Shibuya-ku, tel: 03 3375 3211, www.sunroute.jp/HotelInfoSVE Right in the heart of downtown Tokyo, within easy walking distance of Shinjuku train station.

BUDGET
New Koyo Hotel, 2-26-13 Nihonzutumi Taitou-ku, 111-0021, tel: 03 3873 0343, www.newkoyo.com Clean and friendly, free Wi-Fi access.

Nikkō
MID-RANGE
Okunikko Konishi Hotel, Yumoto-onsen Nikkō-shi Tochigi, tel: 02 88 62 2416, www.okunikkokonishihotel.com/en Calm spa hotel with full *onsen* facilities. Choice of Western and Japanese rooms.

Tokyo and Kantō at a Glance

BUDGET

Turtle Inn, 2-16 Takumi-chō, Nikkō City, tel: 02 88 53 3168, www.turtle-nikko.com/turtle/index_en.html Good location. Western- or Japanese-style rooms. Meals on request.

WHERE TO EAT

Tokyo

See www.bento.com/tokyofood.html for a comprehensive range of over 1000 restaurant reviews. Tokyo now has more Michelin-starred restaurants than any other city in the world. Department stores, hotels and new developments such as the Marunouchi Building and Roppongi Hills are full of places to eat. Useful chains to know include **Moti** (Indian), **Sushisei** (sushi), **Wired** (cafés with internet access) and **Monsoon Café** (Modern Asian).

Nezucafe, Omotesando, Minami-Aoyama 6-5-1, tel: 03 3400 2536. Airy restaurant with pretty view over the gardens of the Nezu Museum.

Hotel de Mikuni, 1-18 Wakaba, Shinjuku, tel: 03 3351 3810. Excellent restaurant in an old church, with one of Tokyo's best chefs, Kiyomi Mikuni.

Akasaka Biz Tower, Akasaka 5-3-1, tel: 03 5114 8500. Over 30 cafés, restaurants and bars. Spanish-Catalan restaurant Bikini is particularly good.

Sushi-dai, Tsukiji Fish market, 4-5-1-Tsukiji, Chūō-ku, tel: 03 3452 1111. Fresh sushi breakfast in the barrack buildings in front of the market.

Tomoegata, 1-7-11 Ryōgoku (near Ryōgoku Station). Chanko Nabe in Sumō land. Very filling. Inexpensive.

Kyubei, Ginza 8-7-6, tel: 03 3571 6523. Some of the most sought-after sushi in Tokyo. Closed Sundays.

Yūrakuchō, cheap yakitori stalls under the Yamanote Line at Yūrakuchō Station.

Yokohama

Yokohama Station mall, MM 21 and Chinatown all have a huge choice.

Daidaiya, Minato-mirai 2-3, Queen's Square, tel: 04 5228 5035. Asian fusion food with views of the harbour.

Kamakura

The Komachi-dōri area inexpensive Japanese restaurants.

SHOPPING

American Pharmacy, B1F, Marunouchi Building, 2-4-1 Marunouchi. Pharmacists speak English.

Meguro Dori, the new destination for interior design devotees. A maze of small furniture boutiques and upscale design stores.

Kinokuniya Bookstore
Takashimaya Times Square Annexe, Shinjuku. Foreign-language book selection. Also **Maruzen** in Nihombashi.

Oriental Bazaar, 5-9-13 Jingū-mae (halfway down Omote Sandō). Ideal for gifts, from kimono to ceramics. Closed Thursdays.

Flea Markets: **Tōgō Shrine** Harajuku.1st and 4th Sundays each month, dawn till dusk. For old kimono, ceramics, etc.

TOURS AND EXCURSIONS

Japan Travel Bureau, tel: 03 5796 5454 for Sunrise Tours with English guide in Tokyo. Also Kamakura, Tokyo Disneyland and others.

USEFUL CONTACTS

JNTO Tourist Information Centre, 10F, Tokyo Kōtsu Kaikan Building, 2-10-1 Yūra-kūchō, Chiyoda-ku, 100-0005, tel: 03 3201 3331, www.jnto.go.jp/eng/ 09:00–17:00, Mon–Fri; 09:00–12:00, Sat. **Narita International Airport**, (main office Terminal 2, branch office Terminal 1) tel: 04 7634 6251, www.narita-airport.jp/en/ Open 09:00–20:00.

American Express, toll-free tel: 0120 02 0120.

Teletourist Service, tel: 03 3201 2911, 24-hour taped information in English; **Japan Travel Phone**, tel: 03 3201 3331, for English advice on public transport; **Ticket Pia**, tel: 03 5237 9966, English telephone booking for sporting events, concerts, theatre, etc.

Tokyo Medical Information Service, tel: 03 5285 8181. Helps locate medical services; for emergency interpreting, tel: 03 5285 8185.

Tokyo Medical Clinic, 32 Mori Building, 3-4-30 Shiba Kōen, Minato-ku, tel: 03 3436 3028. English-speaking doctors.

3
Hokkaidō
and Tōhoku

Hokkaidō is still very much Japan's final frontier: Siberia meets Pennsylvania with a dash of Provence. In winter, drift ice freezes the **Sea of Okhotsk** and **top ski resorts** swing into action. In summer, there are vistas of rolling farmland, greenhouses, Dutch barns and, around Furano and Bibaushi, lavender and sunflower fields.

It is, however, as if Hokkaidō is in search of its soul. The **Ainu** heritage has long been reduced to museum status, and elevating the northern fox to a cute souvenir logo has failed to fill the cultural and spiritual void.

Nevertheless, there is walking and wildlife, as well as volcanoes, lakes, plenty of *onsen* and the best milk, butter and seafood in Japan. **Rebun** and **Rishiri** islands and the **Shiretoko Peninsula** are unmanicured; **Sapporo** is a gourmet's paradise and **Hakodate** is an appealing 19th-century treaty port. Two of the best displayed collections of Ainu textiles, jewellery and utensils are in the **Nibutani Ainu Culture Museum** and the **Hakodate City Museum of Northern Peoples**.

Tōhoku, comprising the six northernmost prefectures of Honshū, has always been maligned as Japan's backyard, which is precisely its attraction. This is unpackaged Japan, with **local crafts** and **festivals** galore, medicinal *onsen* and mountains that retain vestiges of religious significance. The backwater of Hiraizumi in Iwate Prefecture has had the last laugh on the imperial courtiers of the 12th century who viewed the provinces with such disdain, for it, not Kyoto, boasts the single most dazzling treasure left from the Heian Period – the **Golden Hall of Chūson-ji**.

DON'T MISS

★★★ Rebun and Rishiri islands: summer flora.
★★★ Shiretoko National Park: wild coast and waterfall.
★★★ Chūson-ji: small exquisite Golden Hall dates from 1124.
★★ Hakodate: 19th-century treaty port where Japan first encountered Russia.
★★ Sapporo Snow Festival: ice-sculpture extravaganzas.
★★ Osore-zan: volcanic Buddhist cosmos where the souls of dead children wander.
★★ Dewa-sanzan: pilgrimage site of the *yamabushi*.

Opposite: *Rausu-dake on the Shiretoko Peninsula is a popular day-hike.*

CLIMATE

Hokkaidō has a **subarctic** climate. The first snows arrive as early as mid-October, though winter does not kick in until late November. The average winter temperature is below zero; snowfall accumulates to around 5m (16ft). Northern Honshū follows much the same pattern. The thaw begins by mid-April. Summers are more temperate than on the Pacific Coast, with cooler evenings. Autumn is short but has pleasant temperatures.

Opposite: *The Historical Village of Hokkaidō is a depiction of the island's pioneering past.*

SAPPORO

Until the Meiji Period, Hokkaidō was known as Ezo. Then, in the 1870s, the new government decided to open up Japan's equivalent of America's Wild West. Numerous foreign experts were brought in to help develop agriculture and industry. One adviser proposed establishing a small settlement laid out on a **grid pattern**. Sapporo, as it was called, now has a population of approximately 1.87 million, the 5th largest in Japan.

Sapporo's broad avenues and open skyline are somewhat low-key after Tokyo. The main attractions in town relate to the pioneering past as well as eating, drinking and the nightlife in Susukino. No visit to Sapporo is complete without an outing to the **Sapporo Beer Garden and Museum**. Located close to Sapporo station, it is open 09:00–18:00 with free admission (paid tasting). Near Ōdori Park is the distinctive **Clock Tower** building dating from 1878 (the only remaining Russian-style building in the city, open 09:00–17:00, Tuesday–Sunday; admission fee ¥200), and the **Old Hokkaidō Government Building**, a red brick structure typical of the Meiji Period. The **Botanical Gardens** are a pleasant place for a wander (open 09:00–16:00, Tue–Sun); the small **Ainu Museum** in the grounds has an interesting, labelled collection. Open 09:00–16:30, Tue–Sun. Closed in winter. Admission ¥400.

Sapporo's real claim to fame is its spectacular **Snow Festival** which is held from 5 to 11 February in Ōdori Park. Over the past 50 years it has grown into a **sculptural extravaganza** of ice palaces, dinosaurs and statues, many made by the Self Defense Forces (Jieitai),

Sapporo map

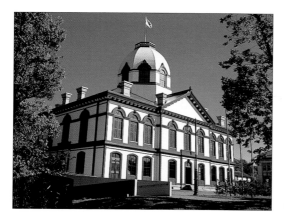

although these days more and more 'unofficial' teams build snow sculptures (both tourists and locals). The festival itself (**Yuki Matsuri**) attracts some two million visitors annually.

Historical Village of Hokkaidō ★★★

Just east of Sapporo, in Nopporo Forest Park, is the Historical Village of Hokkaidō. This has around 60 buildings from the late 19th century, ranging from Dr Kondo's Clinic to Yamamoto's Barber Shop and the Hokuseikan Silkworm House. Entry to the nearby **Historical Museum of Hokkaidō** is separate, but worth paying if you want a thorough lesson on Hokkaidō's history. Both the village and museum are open 09:30–16:30, Tuesday–Sunday. Admission ¥500.

AROUND SAPPORO

Noboribetsu Onsen, in the **Shikotsu-Tōya National Park**, is the most popular spa within easy reach of Sapporo. Its waters come from nearby Jigoku-dani (Hell Valley), which is a rather appropriate description of the theme park atmosphere that pervades this resort.

Lake Tōya is highly picturesque, but lives in constant fear of Usu-zan, its explosive volcanic neighbour, which last erupted in 2000. **Shikotsu**, Japan's second deepest lake, is worth a stop in summer and autumn to explore **Koke-no-dōmon**, an extraordinary canyon carpeted in 30

THE AINU

The Ainu (meaning 'human') are probably related to Siberian ethnic minorities such as the Gilyak. Animal spirits (***kamui***, similar to the kami of Shintō) are crucial to Ainu belief, particularly the bear. The **Iyomante** (Bear Sending) festival involves returning the bear's spirit to the land of the gods by ritually killing it and giving thanks for its meat. Discrimination against the Ainu began in the Edo Period. The modern-day fight for Ainu rights was led by **Kayano Shigeru** (1926–2006), who became the first Ainu member of the Diet in 1994 (*see* page 54). He was one of the last native speakers of the Ainu language. Today around 24,000 Ainu live in Hokkaidō (with a further 10,000 living in Tokyo), though virtually all are of mixed blood and are unable to speak the Ainu language. The Japanese government only recognized the rights of the Ainu in 1997 with the Ainu Cultural Promotion Law.

Above: *A majestic ice owl sculpture at the Sapporo Snow Festival.*
Opposite: *Lake Mashū sits in a volcanic crater formed around 7000 years ago. Its waters are famous for their clarity.*

THE DANCING CRANE

The *tanchō* (Japanese crane) is Hokkaidō's most elegant inhabitant, recognizable by its red crest. Unlike the swan, the *tanchō* never leaves Hokkaidō to nest in Siberia. Early last century, the species was feared to have become extinct as a result of the rapid, and sometimes reckless, development of Hokkaidō. However, a few birds were discovered in the marshes of Kushiro in 1924 and a protection campaign began. A population of around 700 now inhabits the marshes designated as the **Kushiro Shitsugen National Park** in 1987. The sight of *tanchō* dancing in courtship rituals has become the stuff of television wildlife documentaries all over the world.

---

different kinds of moss, just 15km (9 miles) to the southwest of Shikotsu-kohan.

Nibutani Ainu Culture Museum ★★

Biratori, east of Tomakomai, offers the most worthwhile experience of Ainu culture outside Sapporo or Hakodate. The **Nibutani Ainu Culture Museum** is a modern, spacious building with clear and interesting explanations. Open 09:00–16:30 (closed mid-December to mid-January). The **Kayano Shigeru Ainu Memorial Museum** across the road is cramped and delightfully higgledy-piggledy. Open 09:00–16:30, April–November. The Ainu buildings in the garden are also worth seeing.

WINTER HOKKAIDŌ AND THE NATIONAL PARKS

Niseko, 100km (62 miles) southwest of Sapporo is one of Japan's top **ski** and **snowboarding** resorts with three main areas; **Niseko Hirafu** (www.niseko-hirafu.com) is the biggest and the best. Other top resorts east of Sapporo include **Furano**, **Sahoro** and **Rusutsu**. A new ski resort, the Hanazono, has opened recently on the east side of Niseko Hirafu. It is still being further developed and is spearheading a huge tourism drive (*see* www.skihanazono.com). The ski slopes on Hokkaidō tend to be less crowded than on Honshū and there are many ski packages available from Tokyo.

The Abashiri Okhotsk Drift Ice Festival takes place in early Febuary, when it is also possible to navigate the lake on an ice-breaker and see the **drift ice** at close quarters.

Hokkaidō has five national parks, vast areas of spectacular scenery that attract millions of visitors each year. **Daisetsuzan** is the largest, and offers excellent hiking.

Rishiri-Rebun-Sarobetsu National Park ★★★

Neither Cape Soya, nor Wakkanai (Japan's northernmost town) are worth the long drive from Sapporo, but the islands of Rebun and Rishiri are a different matter. Rebun is flat, low and full of flowers in July. On Rishiri, most people's goal is to climb Rishiri-zan, the 1719m (5640ft) volcanic cone at the centre of the island. The 17.6km (11-mile) route takes a full day and you must be fully equipped with water and appropriate clothing. *Minshuku* (B&Bs) and youth hostels are the main lodgings here.

Daisetsuzan National Park ★★

Hokkaidō's biggest national park brims with alpine flora in summer and russet-yellows in autumn; it also, unfortunately, suffers from large tour groups. The main natural attractions of **Sōunkyō Gorge** and plunging waterfalls are much prettier than the resort of Sōunkyō Onsen itself. **Asahi-dake Onsen** is the best base for tackling Asahi-dake, Hokkaidō's highest mountain at 2290m (7513ft).

Akan National Park ★

Akan has three principal lakes and two volcanoes. Akan-kohan, the main resort on Lake Akan, is horribly touristy, though the lake's velvety **marimo** have a certain fascination. Lake Kussaharō is slightly less developed and has a cluster of *onsen*. Nearby Io-zan (Sulphur Mountain) is another of Japan's tourist traps.

In good weather, **Lake Mashū** is a sparkling caldera of deep azure. But it dulls quickly when the mists roll in, a reminder why the Ainu called it Devil's Lake. It is worthwhile paying a visit to the **Akankohan Eco Museum Centre** where there is good information available on walking trails.

MARIMO

Marimo is a spherical species of algae (*Cladophora sauteri*) first discovered in 1823 by Dr Anton Sauter. The marimo found in **Lake Akan** are the largest and roundest in the world, up to 20–30cm (8–12in) in diameter. Hokkaidō is so proud of its marimo that it designated the species a **National Treasure** in 1921. This inadvertently sparked a mania that has never quite died down; tourists still buy baby marimo to keep like pets. For additional scientific information, take a boat trip out to the Marimo Exhibition and Observation Centre. *See* http://marimo-web.org/en

Shiretoko National Park ★★★

In Ainu, Shiretoko means 'the end of the earth'. The Shiretoko Peninsula has also been the end of Japan since 1945, when Russia began its occupation of the bleak Kuril Islands beyond. Despite Japan's demands to return the so-called Northern Territories, the row over sovereignty continues.

Utoro is a better base than

Rausu, though neither port is very attractive. The Shiretoko Nature Centre north of Utoro is worth visiting for its Big Vision film, with swooping aerial views of the Shiretoko area. Shiretoko is where bears come out of hibernation in spring to eat herbs on the coastal cliffs, but **foxes** and **deer** are more common. Open 08:00–17:40 in summer, and 09:00–16:00 in winter. Admission price ¥500. *See* www.shiretoko.or.jp/en/facilities

The star attraction, up a dirt road northwards, is Kamuiwakka-no-taki, a series of pools fed by a warm waterfall that eventually tumbles into the sea. The best way to reach the pools is to walk barefoot in the water up the rock bed, which affords a surprisingly good grip.

HAKODATE

In 1869 Hakodate witnessed the last stand of Tokugawa forces against the new Meiji government at **Goryōkaku**, Japan's sole Western-style fort built, originally, to keep the Russians at bay. The ride up the hideous viewing tower to see the fort's star-shaped remains, however, is not really worth the charge.

The best night view of town is from the top of the Mount Hakodate Ropeway. (In daylight the alternative is a pleasant, though lengthy, walk up through the forest.)

The town's most striking landmark is the **Russian Orthodox Church**. Built in 1916, its onion dome still marks the spiritual home of around 100 households.

Hakodate still feels like a frontier town; it is also completely hooked on fish. At dawn the *asaichi* (morning market) bursts into life in arcades and alleyways near the station; hairy crabs, squid and octopus vie for

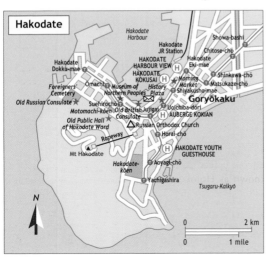

space with king-sized *daikon* (radishes), pink apples and pre-packaged pickles. The docks are the best place to find fresh seafood restaurants. In the 19th-century colonial **Motomachi** area, the old Meiji post office building and warehouses have now been developed into the Hakodate History Plaza, a waterfront complex mildly reminiscent of those in San Francisco or Cape Town. A few other distinctive buildings include the **Old Public Hall of Hakodate Ward** and the **Old British Consulate**, which functioned until 1934. The **Hakodate City Museum of Northern Peoples** in the old Bank of Japan building has some of the best Ainu textiles and objects in Hokkaidō.

Around the plaza are plenty of shops, restaurants and entertainment (*see* www.hakodate-kanemori.com/en).

Above: *Statues of Jizō, saviour of children, at the sacred site of Osore-zan.*

NORTHERN TŌHOKU

Aomori City is the gateway to an eponymous prefecture that has a lot to offer. **Hirosaki** is a pleasant castle town with a lively Nebuta Festival (*see* panel, page 60). **Lake Towada**, located in the Towada-Hachimantai National Park, is famous for its tranquil waters, magnificent colours and appalling traffic jams during summer and autumn. **Morioka**, the capital of Iwate Prefecture, is a spacious city with one or two good craft shops in the older parts of town. Its culinary speciality is Wanko-soba, small bowls of noodles, which you are supposed to consume in volume.

Osore-zan ★★

The remote Shimokita Peninsula is home to Osore-zan (Mountain of Terror), an 879m-high (2884ft) volcano. It is also an attractive place to explore by car, particularly the rocky section of coast known as Hotoke-ga-Ura (Buddha Inlet).

Like Kōya-san, Osore-zan is a site which is sacred to the dead – in this case specifically the souls of children. The tell-tale signs are the countless windswept statues of **Jizō** (the saviour of children). From the temple of Entsū-ji a

SEIKAN TUNNEL

Travelling from Hakodate to Aomori by train is mildly disturbing. After all, what if an earthquake hits when you are travelling 787ft (240m) below sea level? The Seikan Tunnel opened in 1988 after 17 years under construction. It carries the world's deepest railway line and, at 53.85km (33.5 miles), is also the **world's longest tunnel**, although it may be overtaken by the Gotthard Base Tunnel under construction in Switzerland (due for completion in 2018), at 57km (35.4 miles). There are two stations in the Seikan Tunnel, one at either coast line. To disembark for a tour, you must book on one of the slower trains and specify in advance.

Above: *Rickshaws have seen a revival with the increasing tourist trade.*

path leads across a volcanic Buddhist cosmos past sites with names such as Endless Hell. The destination is **Paradise Beach**, a strip of sand lapped by the rippling waves of a lake. From beyond the grave, toddlers must navigate this tricky terrain with the help of Jizō.

Twice a year (from 20–24 July and 9–11 October), blind women **mediums** (*itako*) gather to help parents contact their dead children in a shamanistic ritual of ancient origins tinged with modern-day overtones.

Kakunodate ★★

Kakunodate, situated between Morioka and Akita, is best known for its broad avenue of old samurai houses (*Buke Yashiki*). The **Aoyagi House**, built in 1860, is particularly well worth visiting; it has a warren of museums featuring everything from an old gramophone collection to samurai armour. Open 09:00–17:00, admission free. The town is compact enough to explore on foot with the aid of a map available at the tourist information centre next to the station.

Tōno, southeast of Morioka, is best known for its ghost tales immortalized in 1910 in the book *The Legends of Tōno* by Yanagita Kunio. In the Tōno Valley are several old *magariya* (L-shaped) farmhouses and folk villages, all very much on the tourist trail.

Hachimantai Plateau ★★

The Hachimantai Plateau, bordering Akita Prefecture, is a wild, **lunar landscape** of hot springs and walking opportunities that represents the very antithesis of packaged Japan. This is where the *onsen* connoisseur goes for serious medicinal therapy: **Tamagawa Onsen** (*see* www.tamagawa-onsen.jp) on the Tama River is a miasmic maze of mud and steam as well as water; **Goshogake** is another miracle of sauna baths and heated vents.

ARTS AND CRAFTS

Morioka is particularly famous for its Nambu *tetsubin* (**iron kettles**) made by master craftsmen. These need not break the bank, but will certainly weigh down your luggage. Kakunodate's speciality is *kabazaiku* (items made from **cherry bark**, e.g. tea caddies and baskets). *Kokeshi* (tall, painted wooden dolls) made their debut probably in the 18th century and are made all over Tōhoku in slightly different styles. Most prefectures have their own lacquer traditions. Probably the most renowned is Aizu lacquer (from Fukushima), which features the gold sprinkling technique known as *maki-e*.

Hiraizumi

As the 12th-century stronghold of the northern Fujiwara clan, Hiraizumi merits a visit for its temple complexes and Jōdo Garden. Most buildings have either disappeared over the centuries or been rebuilt, but the past lives on in the splendid Golden Hall of **Chūson-ji**. At one point Chuson-ji was even considered a rival to Kyoto.

Chūson-ji ★★★

Founded in the 9th century, all the present buildings are from the 17th century, except the **Golden Hall** (**Konjiki-dō**), which dates from 1124. Having nearly survived earthquakes and fires for nearly 900 years, this architectural wonder is now housed behind plated glass in a concrete fortress.

The Golden Hall is the rather small, but exquisite mausoleum of four generations of Fujiwaras, buried beneath a central **Amida Buddha** flanked by an array of heavenly attendants. The entire creation is a dazzling display of gold leaf and mother-of-pearl inlay, believed by some scholars to have inspired Marco Polo's reference to 'all the gold in Cipangu'.

A fraction of Chūson-ji's 3000 treasures are kept in a separate hall, which houses among others an outstanding image of the Thousand-armed Kannon.

The temple grounds are particularly famous for their autumn colours.

Mōtsū-ji and Jōdo Garden ★★

Mōtsū-ji has Japan's best preserved Heian garden. In its 12th-century heyday, the estate comprised 40 pagodas and countless buildings, including a copy of the Byōdō-in of Uji. Now only foundations remain. The gardens feature a large lake with strategically placed islands. The most spectacular time to visit is in late June, when 30,000 irises come into bloom. The temple has a youth hostel which is worth staying in.

THE TRAGIC HERO

*In the summer grass
lie the soldiers
and their dreams.*
Matsuo Bashō (1644–94)
In 1189, the tyrannical Minamoto Yoritomo, first *shōgun* of Japan, turned against his brother, **Yoshitsune**, who had successfully steered the Minamoto to victory at the Battle of Danno-ura. Yoshitsune fled to Hiraizumi with his faithful servant, Benkei, and took shelter with Fujiwara Hidehira, the grandson of Kiyohira (*see page 13*). Yoshitsune was betrayed by Hidehira's son, however, and ended up committing suicide to evade capture. The **Takatachi Gikei-dō**, a small shrine marking the spot, looks rather insignificant. Yet it was here that Yoshitsune earned immortality in Japanese literature and legend as the tragic hero.

Below: *The Heian Period garden of Mōtsū-ji.*

Takkoku-no-Iwaya ★★

Takkoku-no-Iwaya is approximately 30 minutes by bicycle
(10 minutes by taxi) from Hiraizumi. Once used as refuge
during the 9th century, the cave is now concealed by a
charming building on stilts reminiscent of Kiyomizu-dera
in Kyoto. Carved in the rock face nearby is an unusually
large Buddha image.

SOUTHERN TŌHOKU

Sendai, known for its silk, is the *kokeshi* capital of Tōhoku
(*see* panel, page 58) and also its largest city, closely associated with the Date family that ruled it during the Edo
Period. Allied bombing raids in 1945 somehow spared the
exuberant **Ōsaki Hachiman-jinja** built by Date Masamune
in 1607.

Most people pass through Sendai to go to **Matsushima**
(Pine Islands), immortalized by the 17th-century poet
Bashō in his famous work *The Narrow Road to the Deep
North*. Matsushima is one of Japan's three great scenic
spots, but the bay is also a tourist trap.

Zaō, west of Sendai and southeast of Yamagata City, is
Tōhoku's top ski and *onsen* resort area, renowned for its
plateau of fir trees which, in winter, turn into *juhyō* (snow
monsters) covered in spiky layers of hoar frost.

Dewa-sanzan (Three Mountains of Dewa) ★★

Dewa-sanzan in Yamagata Prefecture has long been a
prime destination for *yamabushi*, ascetic practitioners of
Shugen-dō, a blend of esoteric Buddhism and Shinto. The

pilgrimage season, from July to
September, has seen an increase in
visitors since the economic un-
certainties of the 1990s.

Of the three peaks, **Mount Haguro**
represents birth, **Mount Gassan** (the
highest at 1984m/6510ft) represents
death, and **Mount Yudono** (1500m/
4922ft) rebirth. At 414m (1358ft),
Mount Haguro is the most accessible,
either by bus or via 2446 steps. It is

also the only one of the three that is open year-round. Both scenery and shrines improve along the circuit (nowadays buses help those who don't wish to walk all the way). Alternatively, *yamabushi* courses are offered for those who want to gain a fuller insight into asceticism. The techniques used for this include bathing under a cold waterfall.

Bandai-kōgen ★★

Bandai-kōgen, northeast of Aizu-Wakamatsu, is more immediately attractive than the somewhat mysterious territory of Hachimantai. Dotted with lakes, the area provides excellent walking opportunities in summer and skiing in winter.

Aizu Wakamatsu is a feudal town which is best known for its *Byakkotai* (League of White Tigers) who needlessly committed suicide in defence of their lord in the run-up to the Meiji Restoration.

SADO ISLAND

Though strictly speaking part of Central Honshū, the island of Sado spiritually belongs to the provincial heritage of Tōhoku. For centuries Sado was a place to exile political troublemakers, whom the Tokugawa *shōgun*s used to extract gold from Sado's mines.

This island of rice paddies and fishing villages can be explored in a couple of days. These days it is best known for the **Kodo Drummers**. In the third week of August, the Kodo community hosts an 'Earth Celebration' arts festival in Ogi.

Opposite: *Takkoku-no-Iwaya lies off the beaten track.*

KODO DRUMMERS

In 1971 a group of musicians founded a community on Sado which evolved into the Kodo Drummers, meaning **'Children of the Drum'**. Today, the group takes up to thirty drums, of which the largest is the Ō-taiko, on its world tours. Although many pieces of Kodo music are modern, several classical Japanese instruments are used for accompaniment.

Hokkaidō and Tōhoku at a Glance

BEST TIMES TO VISIT

Hokkaidō and most of **Tōhoku** are snow-bound between Nov and March. Late May–July is the best time to see the flora. **June** is a very popular time to visit Hokkaidō because it lies beyond the reach of the rainy season. Always make reservations in summer and autumn.

GETTING THERE

Hokkaidō

Daily **flights** service Sapporo (New Chitose), Hakodate, Asahikawa and Memanbetsu from Haneda, Kansai International and Nagoya. It takes about 11 hours from Tokyo to Sapporo on the **Tōhoku Shinkansen** via Morioka, and north via the Seikan Tunnel on JR's limited express services. This is worth it for JR pass holders; otherwise rail is not price competitive with air. **Ferry** services are an option between Aomori (or Ōma) and Hakodate, or between Tokyo and Tomakomai.

Tōhoku

Sendai, Niigata, Morioka and Aomori are all serviced by **domestic** and **international air** connections. The Tōhoku, Yamagata, Akita and Niigata **Shinkansen** lines all provide an excellent, fast rail service. Apart from the Aomori-Hakodate link, a **ferry** service runs from Niigata to Otaru and ferry and hydrofoil services from Niigata to Sado Island.

GETTING AROUND

Hokkaidō

There are daily **flights** from Sapporo to Wakkanai, Asahikawa, Hakodate and Memanbetsu, and from Wakkanai to Rebun and Rishiri (also serviced by ferry from Wakkanai). **JR** services connect Hakodate and Sapporo with Wakkanai in the north and all major towns in the centre and east, but **car hire** offers the most flexibility. **Sapporo** and **Hakodate** have good subway and **tram** systems, respectively. Sapporo also has a bus service operated by Hokkaido Chuo Bus, tel: 011 231 0500. A ¥750 one-day bus pass will take you around the sights.

Tōhoku

A **JR pass** wins hands down on the Shinkansen and local JR routes. Morioka is a good base for **Kakunodate** and **Hachimantai**. Hiring a car is the most efficient way to explore Hachimantai, Bandai-kōgen and also the Shimokita Peninsula. To get to **Osore-zan** by public transport, go by JR to Nōhei-ji from Aomori or Morioka. Change at Nōhei-ji for Shimokita Station (Mutsu) and then take the private Ohata line to Tanabu Station. Buses from Tanabu to Osore-zan run April–end October only. For **Hiraizumi**, take the Shinkansen to Ichinoseki and then transfer to a local train or bus. Hire a **bicycle** next door to the station to see the sights.

For **Dewa-sanzan** go by JR from Akita or Niigata to Tsuruoka, then by bus.

WHERE TO STAY

Sapporo
LUXURY

Cross Hotel Sapporo, 23 Kita-2 jo Nishi 2, Saporro 060-0002, tel: 011 272 0010, www.crosshotel.com Elegant, well located hotel.
Hotel New Ōtani Sapporo, N2, W1, Chūō-ku, tel: 011 222 1111. Just about the most luxurious in town. Near Ōdōri Park.

MID-RANGE

Nakamuraya Ryokan, N3, W7, Chūō-ku, tel: 011 241 2111, www.nakamura-ya. com/english.html Near the Botanical Gardens.

Daisetsuzan
BUDGET

Choyotei Ryokan, Sōunkyō Onsen, Kamikawa-chō, Kamikawa-gun, Hokkaido. Located on the northeastern, most developed part of the park, near the Sōunkyō Gorge. This makes a great spot for starting walks, and is a perfect place to come back to with aching limbs, as it has its own hot springs.

Shiretoko
MID-RANGE

Shiretoko Grand Hotel, Shari-chō, Utoro, tel: 01522 4 3222, www.shiretoko.co.jp/english/index.html Large hotel with roof-top *onsen*.

Hokkaidō and Tōhoku at a Glance

Hakodate
MID-RANGE
Ichinomatsu's Ryokan, 3-17 Yunokawa-chō, Hakodate-shi tel: 0138 57 0001, www. ichinomatsu.co.jp/english Luxury *ryokan* with 29 rooms, plus indoor and outdoor *onsen*.

Tōhoku, Shimokita Peninsula
MID-RANGE
Grandeco Hotel, Aza-arasuna-sawayama, Oaza-Hibara, Kitashiobara-mura, Yama-gun, Fukushima 969-2701, tel: 0241 32 3200. In a more rural location, but not far from Fukushima. Great *onsen* and lovely views.
Hotel New Yagen, 6-1 Aza Yagen, Ōhata machi, Shimokita-gun, Aomori Prefecture 039-4401, tel: 0175 34 3311, www.new yagen.com *Ryokan* convenient for Osore-zan, especially by car.

Morioka
MID-RANGE
Ryokan Kumagai, 3-2-5, Oosawakawara, Morioka City, tel: 0196 51 3020, http:// kumagairyokan.com Pretty Japanese-style inn, close to the museum and art gallery in the centre of town.
Hachimantai Goshogake Onsen Hotel, Kumazawa Kokyūrin-nai, Hachimantai, Kazuno City, Akita Prefecture, tel: 0186 31 2221. An old-fashioned experience for geothermal devotees.

Hokkaidō-Sapporo
There are lots of good restaurants around the Susukino area.
Sapporo Beer Garden, N7, E9, Sapporo City, tel 011 742 1531. All-you-can-eat *jingisukan*, in three vast halls. Reservations recommended.
Ramen Yokocho, Minami 5, Nishi 3. A 'ramen alley' which is bustling and great fun.

Hakodate
Many of the small eateries near the morning market – such as the **West Wharf**, tel: 013 824 8108 – serve *rāmen* with a whole crab on top.

Tōhoku-Morioka
Hanaotome, Kita Kanjo Sen, Sendai, tel: 022 772 3011. Traditional Japanese restaurant with good range of beautifully presented food.

Kakunodate
Sakura Tei, Yokomachi 18, tel: 0187 53 2970. Tatami-mats set the scene at this lovely traditional restaurant.

Morioka has several old *Meiji*-style shops. One good area is **Konya-chō** (Dyers' Quarter), across Naka-no-hashi and left

just after the old Iwate Bank Building. Look out for Shirasawa Sembei (home-made rice crackers) and Kamasada Kōbō (iron kettles).

Hokkaidō
Hokkaidō and Sapporo Tourist Information, North (kita) 6, West (nishi) 4, in JR Sapporo Station bl. West Concourse (1st floor), tel: 011 213 5088.
Skiing: www.snowjapan.com Most comprehensive source of skiing and snowboarding information, resort reviews, and places to stay. For tours to Niseko, Japan's snowboarding capital, *see* www.snowave.com

Sapporo
Sapporo English Assistance Line, tel: 011 222 4894
Nippon Rent-a-car, tel: 011 746 0919.
Morioka
Morioka Tourist Information Center, JR Morioka Station, tel: 019 625 2090.
Eki Rent-a-car, 019 624 5212.
Tōhoku
Ideha Cultural Centre, Haguro-machi, tel: 0235 62 4727, fax: 62 4729. Dewasanzan *yamabushi* courses. Serious applicants only.

SAPPORO	J	F	M	A	M	J	J	A	S	O	N	D
AVERAGE TEMP. °C	-5	-4	0	6	12	16	20	22	17	11	4	-1
AVERAGE TEMP. °F	23	25	32	43	54	61	68	72	63	52	39	30
RAINFALL mm	107	94	82	62	55	66	69	142	138	116	99	100
RAINFALL in	4.2	3.7	3.2	2.4	2.2	2.6	2.7	5.6	5.4	4.6	3.9	3.9
DAYS OF RAINFALL	21	13	13	9	10	5	12	7	8	14	15	16

4
Central Honshū

In the days of the Tokugawa *shōguns*, the Tōkaidō was the busiest highway leading to Edo. Now the traffic tends to flow the other way, and with good reason: **Fuji-Hakone-Izu National Park** combines the best views of Mount Fuji with the opportunity to soak in an *onsen*, and a dose of nostalgia, for this is the land immortalized in Hiroshige's *Fifty-three Stations of the Tōkaidō* and Hokusai's *Thirty-six Views of Mount Fuji*.

Disregard the big resorts and you can glimpse history. In the Kiso Valley you can even live it at some of the old post stations on the Nakasendō road.

The Japanese love nature, and they love it most passionately in the **Japan Alps**, where **alpine flora** and *onsen* abound. Until the Meiji Restoration mountains were sacred, to be tackled purely for purposes of pilgrimage. The concept of climbing for enjoyment came from British missionaries. One of them, William Gowland, actually coined the term 'Japan Alps' in his *Japan Guide* of 1888; another, AC Shaw, 'discovered' the summer resort of Karuizawa on the borders of Nagano. Nowadays, **hiking** and **skiing** are national pastimes pursued with almost religious fervour.

Nagano Prefecture is less than two hours from Tokyo on the Hokuriku Shinkansen line completed for the Winter Olympics in 1998. Both Nagano City and **Matsumoto** offer cultural diversions en route to the ski slopes. Beyond the Alps, **Kanazawa**, with its justifiably famous garden of **Kenroku-en**, is one of Japan's top attractions, as is the rustic **Noto Peninsula**.

Opposite: *Matsumoto Castle, imposing gateway to the Japan Alps.*

CLIMBING MOUNT FUJI

Nihon (Japan) means 'origin of the sun', so it is appropriate that the goal of climbing Mount Fuji is to see the sun rise. The season lasts from 1 July to 31 August. 'No sleep – tumult all night of parties returning late from the mountain, or arriving for the pilgrimage,' wrote Lafcadio Hearn from his mountain hut at 03:30 on 25 August 1897. Little has changed. Most people drive up to the 5th Station and then walk the remaining six hours to the summit. Climbing Mount Fuji is an institution, not a recipe for enjoyment, though a good sunrise really can make it all worthwhile.

Opposite: *Tourists can sail the length of Lake Ashi on a magnificent galleon.*
Below: *The vermilion torii of Hakone Shrine.*

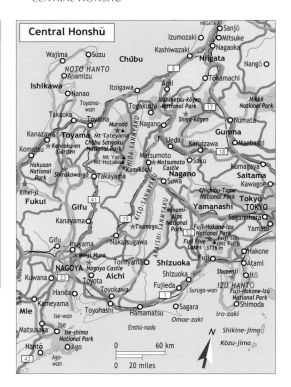

FUJI-HAKONE-IZU NATIONAL PARK

Mount Fuji is rather like Japan itself: it may look reassuringly permanent and pristine from a distance, but that says nothing about the situation beneath the surface. Nevertheless, Fuji's snow-crusted volcanic cone is deservedly one of the world's most instantly recognizable images. 'No wonder that it is a sacred mountain, and so dear to the Japanese...' wrote Isabella Bird as she sailed into Yokohama in 1878.

Hakone ★★

In the Edo Period, Hakone was the site of a major barrier on the **Tōkaidō**. Evading the checkpoint was punishable by death through crucifixion. Today there is a peril-free circular tour from the train terminus of Hakone Yumoto by funicular railway, cable car, pirate ship and bus through this Fuji-viewing region 90km (56 miles) west of Tokyo.

Highlights include **Miyanoshita**, an *onsen* town dominated by the 19th-century **Fujiya Hotel**, whose landlord in the early days objected to Europeans and Americans not having the good grace to take their boots off. Further up the line, the **Hakone Open-Air Museum** (by Chōkoku-no-mori station) offers spacious gardens full of Rodin and Henry Moore sculptures. Open 09:00–17:00; admission ¥1600 (*see* www.hakone-oam.or.jp/english).

Between Sōunzan and Lake Ashi, a cable car passes over the malodorous moonscape of **Ōwakudani**, where it is only too obvious just how close Japan sits to the geological edge (*see* page 6). Here, the Japanese love to hard-boil eggs in sulphurous pools; on clear days, Fuji's cone looms through the steam. Down at Lake Ashi, the views are even better. From here a splendidly tacky pirate ship sails south past the picturesque *torii* of **Hakone Shrine** to the village of Hakone-machi, once the site of the Tōkaidō barrier. A short walk along an avenue of 17th-century Japanese cedar trees takes you to Moto Hakone, from where buses leave for Hakone Yumoto.

Izu Peninsula ★★

A car is useful for exploring this pretty peninsula dotted with *onsen*, as well as ubiquitous (and dubious) theme parks such as **Atagawa Tropical and Alligator Garden**. The big resorts of Dōgashima, on the west coast, and Itō and Atami on the east, hold little attraction; beaches heave in summer. Out of season, however, exploring the coastline down to **Cape Irō** has its rewards, but beware of the many clever, pick-pocketing monkeys at Cape Hagachizaki. Admission ¥1600. You can also take a tourist ferry along this beautiful coastline. The Orchid Resort, in Dogashima on the west coast of Izu, is another great visit. Admission ¥1300, children free.

CLIMATE

The Fuji-Hakone-Izu area has a similar climate to the Kantō region. The Japan Alps provide welcome respite from the heat of the plains in summer and pleasant temperatures in spring and autumn. Winter arrives in mid-November in the Northern Alps and on the Sea of Japan coast. Major routes open up again in late March or April, when the snow thaws. Kanazawa has wet summers and cold winters, but is very pleasant in spring and autumn.

MOA Museum of Art ★★★

Atami is worth lingering in only to see the first-rate MOA Art Museum housed in the headquarters of one of Japan's very wealthy religious sects. Elevators in the cliff face take you up to opulent galleries of oriental ceramics, lacquer and gold worth the admission charge. The museum has great views over the ocean. Open 09:30–16:30 Fri–Wed. Admission ¥1600 (see www.moaart.or.jp/english/top.html).

Shuzenji ★★

Shuzenji Onsen in central Izu has all the usual souvenir shops, but nevertheless retains a definitive old-world charm. Both Shuzenji *onsen* and temple are said to have been founded in AD806 by Kūkai, founder of Kōya-san. Vermilion bridges straddle the Katsura River, lined with *ryokan* (traditional inns) and bath houses. Try taking a dip in **Tokko-no-yu**, an open-air bath carved out of the rock. Not that taking the waters is always fun: 800 years ago the son of Minamoto Yoritomo (*see* panel, page 59) was supposedly poisoned here for plotting treachery.

Even so, Shuzenji remained a firm favourite with 19th-century literary figures like **Kawabata Yasunari**, whose novel, *The Dancing Girl of Izu*, gives this spa town a much less sinister spin.

Shimoda ★★

In 1854, Commodore Perry sailed his black ships into **Shimoda**, a year after his initial foray into Tokyo Bay. At the temple of Ryōsen-ji, he signed the Kanagawa Treaty between the USA and Japan. Shimoda duly became a treaty port. In 1856, Townsend Harris was appointed first American consul. The Ryōsen-ji Museum includes a collection of items that belonged to Harris's *geisha*. Harris took up residence in the grounds of **Gyokusen-ji**, where he spent a frustrating two years trying to get an interview with the *shōgun*. He couldn't have known that trade relations would still be on the political agenda 150 years later. On 17 and 18 May each year there is a **Black Ships Festival** with American and Japanese bands, processions and fireworks. The temple is open 08:00–17:00, admission ¥300.

THE DANCING GIRL OF IZU

In 1968 Kawabata Yasunari (1899–1972) became the first Japanese writer to win the Nobel Prize for literature. His earliest famed work is *The Dancing Girl of Izu*, published in 1926. Virtually semi-biographical, it tells of a high school student who goes off on a walking holiday to Izu and is charmed by a young dancing girl. **Mishima Yukio**, the right-wing novelist who disembowelled himself in 1970, regarded Kawabata as his teacher. Perhaps it was really the other way round: in 1972, Kawabata himself committed suicide, though without an apparent motive.

JAPAN ALPS

The Japan Alps divide into three broad ranges: the **Northern Alps** comprise the dramatic Hida and Tateyama ranges, as well as **major ski resorts** such as Shiga Kōgen; the **Central Alps** (Kiso range) offer great alpine scenery and hiking; the **Southern Alps** (Akaishi range) are less developed and accessible.

Zenkō-ji ★★★

Nagano City's star attraction is the ornate temple of **Zenkō-ji**, traditionally dedicated to the first Buddhist image that arrived from Korea in the 6th century. This gilt-bronze Amida triad is never on view, but a copy is displayed every seven years in spring, when huge crowds come to visit. The next showing will be in 2010. Open 05:30–16:30, admission free.

Zenkō-ji's other big drawcard is finding the '**key to paradise**'. This entails groping along in a pitch black tunnel beneath the temple in search of a handle in the wall at the far end. Emerging into daylight is seen as the equivalent of rebirth, if only because it is such a relief to get out.

Hokusai-kan Museum ★★★

The small town of Obuse, northeast of Nagano, is associated with Takai Kōzan, the Edo merchant who became the patron of the aged, struggling artist **Hokusai**. The Hokusai-kan Museum exhibits the widest range of Hokusai's work in Japan, including woodblock prints, paintings and sketches. It is open 09:00–17:00 in summer, 09:30–16:30 in winter. Admission ¥500.The shop has an extensive range of reproduction prints on sale.

Togakushi ★★

Togakushi, some 20km (12 miles) northwest of Nagano, is a

Below: *Buddhist guardians of Zenkō-ji.*

**TATEYAMA-KUROBE
ALPINE ROUTE**

This popular route runs
90km (56 miles) across the
Northern Alps between
Shinano-ōmachi in Nagano
Prefecture and Toyama on the
Japan Sea. The traditional
combination of funicular railway, bus and train transport,
costing roughly ¥10,000, takes
only 3.5 hours, though rushing
through without stopping to
admire the scenery would be
pointless. Highlights include
the spectacular 186m (610ft)
Kurobe Dam and gorge, views
of sacred **Mount Tateyama**, as
well as hiking opportunities in
the Murodō area, including
the dramatic lake of Mikuriga-
ike. The route is open
between the end of April and
late November. August to
October is the busiest period.
See www.alpen-route.com/
english

ski resort and home to the **Togakushi Minzoku-kan**
museum, which explores the subject of **Ninja** (samurai
masters of stealth). The local Ninja village, **Ninja Mura**,
is touristy but a fun ninja-themed day out. Open 09:00–
17:00, April–November.

Matsumoto Castle ★★★

The town of Matsumoto is dominated by **Karasu-jō**
(Crow's Castle), as its imposing fortification is known.
Karasu-jō has a particularly striking moon-viewing tower
and *donjon* (castle keep), which dates from 1597. Open
08:30–17:00, admission ¥600. In town, **Nakamachi-dōri**,
a street with traditional houses and craft shops, is good
for a browse.

Skiing and *Onsen* Resorts ★★

Most major ski resorts on Honshū are in Nagano and
Niigata prefectures. **Shiga Kōgen**, 20km (13 miles) northeast of Nagano City is the biggest, with 22 areas covered
by one pass. At Jigokudani (Hell Valley) near **Yudanaka**
is the *rotenburo* (open-air bath), reserved exclusively for
Nagano's celebrity, **macaque monkeys**.

Hakuba, which hosted several Winter Olympic events

in 1998, is renowned for its summer
alpine flora. In winter **Happō-one** is
particularly suitable for advanced
and intermediate skiers, with a max-
imum run of 8km (5 miles). The
attractive *onsen* resort of **Nozawa**
has a good mix of easy and advanced
ski runs.

Bessho Onsen, south of Nagano,
is an unassuming resort with
numerous temples dating back to
the Kamakura Period; here you will
find the unique octagonal pagoda
of Anraku-ji. East of Nagano in
Gunma Prefecture is **Hōshi Onsen**,
famous throughout Japan for its
old, wooden bathhouse.

Kamikōchi ★★

This small resort in the Northern Alps is Japan's equivalent of a Swiss resort: exclusive and expensive. **Walter Weston** (1861–1940), the father of Alpine climbing in Japan, first came here in 1891. Since then millions of others have followed. Weston was honoured with the Fourth Class Order of the Sacred Treasure in 1937 and is remembered each June in a festival at the start of the climbing season.

Kamikōchi's appeal is its range of hiking opportunities, from the easiest valley-walking to a popular three-day Alpine traverse between Mount Yari and Mount Hotaka.

Takayama ★★★

The **San-machi suji** area of Takayama is still very much old Japan, crammed with houses, craft shops, temples and small museums. The day always begins with morning markets at Takayama Jinya and by the Miyagawa River.

The best sights include the **Kusakabe Mingei-kan** (Kusakabe Folk Museum) and the **Yoshijima-ke** (Yoshijima Heritage House) next door, formerly the home of a sake merchant. Takayama's heritage of carpentry is visible in every joint. The **Takayama Yatai Kaikan** houses the enormous floats used at festival time (*see* www.hida.jp/english).

If you are unable to see the thatched, *gasshō*-style farmhouses at **Shirakawa-gō** and **Gokayama** (about 2–3 hours northwest of Takayama), go instead to **Hida Folk Village** nearby where there are several magnificent examples. *Gasshō* (joining hands in prayer) is a poetic reference to the steeply angled roof of these structures, designed to stop snow from settling. Open daily, 08:30–17:00, March–November; 08:30–16:30, December–February (open until 20:30, July–August over weekends). Admission fee is ¥700.

Above: *Ritual offerings to the kami include rice, salt, water and, on happy occasions, sake, donated to shrines and temples in large barrels.*
Opposite: *Vibrant, colourful dancing processions mark the Tanabata Festival.*

TAKAYAMA FESTIVALS

Takayama's many festivals draw the crowds, and that makes finding accommodation virtually impossible without reserving well in advance.
• The big **Sannō Festival** (14–15 April) is one of the top three in Japan, famed for its huge floats and extraordinary *karakuri* (**automata**).
• In August there are firework displays, Bon dances and a **Tanabata** (Star) Festival.
• The autumn **Yahata Festival** (9–10 October) is a virtual repeat of the Sannō Festival.

Above: *Apprentice Zen monks – these men choose a highly austere existence.*
Opposite: *The tranquil waters of Kenroku-en.*

CORMORANT FISHING

Ukai (cormorant fishing) is an ancient summer practice mentioned in the 8th-century **Manyō-shū** anthology. Traditionally dressed fishermen sail along in wooden boats decked either side with burning braziers to attract *ayu* (sweetfish) to the surface. Each fisherman handles several cormorants on reins. Each bird has a ring around its neck to prevent it from swallowing the fish. To go out on a boat and watch this spectacle is magical. The Kiso River at **Inuyama** and the Nagara River at Gifu are both famous *ukai* venues, as are Arashiyama in Kyoto, the **Shimanto River** in Shikoku and **Iwakuni** in Yamaguchi Prefecture.

AROUND NAGOYA

Nagoya has little to recommend it apart from the **Tokugawa Art Museum**, if you have a few hours to spare. This has a huge collection of objects from the Owari branch of the Tokugawa family, including the fabled 12th-century scroll of *The Tale of Genji* (usually displayed in reproduction form only). Open 10:00–17:00, admission ¥1200. *See* www.tokugawa-art-museum.jp/english/index.html

Also worth a quick visit is **Nagoya Castle**. Open 09:00–16:30, admission ¥500. The dock area has also been recently renovated, and has an excellent aquarium plus an **Antartic Museum**, housed in a ship that was used in Antartic missions. Open 09:30–17:00, admission ¥2400 yen (combo ticket including aquarium, antartic museum and other facilities in the dock area).

Inuyama ★★

Inuyama Castle at Inuyama, north of the Kiso River, has one of Japan's oldest *donjons*. Inuyama's other claim to fame is the garden of **Uraku-en**, which contains Jo-an, a tea house built in 1618 by the brother of Oda Nobunaga (*see* page 14). This National Treasure is admired for its sophisticated rusticity. Open year round.

Meiji Mura ★★

Meiji Mura, near Inuyama, is an outdoor museum of Meiji (and Taishō) Period architecture and is much larger than Sapporo's Hokkaidō Historical Village. The highlight is the Frank Lloyd Wright-designed façade of the original Imperial Hotel in Tokyo, which withstood the 1923 earthquake, but ended up being dismantled anyway. *See* www.meijimura.com/english/index.html

Old Nakasendō Staging Posts ★★★

Tsumago and **Magome** are two old staging posts along the Nakasendō, where feudal lords once quaffed the finest sake on their way to Edo. Magome is the birthplace of the novelist Shimazaki Tōson (1872–1943) and Tsumago is virtually a samurai film set, faithfully restored in 1968.

The 2–3 hour walk between Magome and Tsumago, over the Magome Pass, is probably one of the most pleasant in Japan and highly recommended. Both these villages have good *minshuku*-style accommodation, which serve to make a stay in provincial Edo that much more authentic.

KANAZAWA AND BEYOND

Kanazawa escaped allied bombing raids in 1945 and it shows. By the late 17th century, this stylish castle town already had a population of 70,000, making it larger than Nagoya at the time; the Ōmichō market, has now bustled with activity for three centuries.

Under the Maeda family, the Kaga region, as it was then known, developed its own highly distinctive arts and crafts. Kanazawa is particularly *gaijin*-friendly as a result of the many cultural exchange programmes it runs. Most sights are compact enough to see on foot.

Kenroku-en ★★★

Kenroku-en is considered to be the most pleasing of Japan's top three landscaped gardens. It was begun in 1676, in the outer grounds of Kanazawa Castle, as the **Lotus Pond Garden** of the fifth Maeda lord; by 1837 it had taken on its present form.

Garden-planning in Japan is a highly developed aesthetic. The very name **Kenroku** (Six Virtues) is a reference to a 16th-century Chinese gardening manual, which advocated that a garden should have **six features**: spaciousness, seclusion, an artificial element, an air of antiquity, running water and extensive views.

Kenroku-en is a textbook example. It covers 10ha (25 acres), yet is a world unto itself. It comprises tea houses, ponds, streams, waterfalls and views towards the Sea of Japan; its prize artificial element is a two-legged stone lantern, one foot in and one foot out of Misty Pond. Tour groups are a significant hazard throughout the year, but tranquillity is not hard to come by early or late in the day.

EIHEI-JI

Eihei-ji in Fukui Prefecture is the headquarters of the **Sōtō** sect of **Zen Buddhism**, founded in 1244. Sōtō has 8 million members and is also active overseas. Eihei-ji is large, peaceful and surrounded by ancient cedar trees. Inevitably it is on the tour group trail, but it also has a very active meditation centre, which will accept genuinely interested outsiders wanting to try a short Zen programme. For more information or to make reservations at Eihei-ji or other Sōtō Zen temples, check out: http://global.sotozen-net.or.jp

KAGA ARTS AND CRAFTS

The Kanazawa region is known for a number of specific crafts all of which are colourful and exuberant. The history of **Wajima lacquerware** on the Noto Peninsula goes back 1000 years; even today Wajima City has hundreds of workshops. The art of **Kaga Yūzen**, a traditional form of hand-dyeing, is over 300 years old. Five classic colours are used: indigo, dark red, ochre, green and purple. **Kutani** ware, a gaudy form of pottery revived in the 19th century, uses the same palette. Another of Kanazawa's claims to fame is that it produces virtually all the **gold leaf** used in Japan.

Opposite: *Women display their produce at the Wajima morning market.*
Below: *Senmaida, an intricate maze of rice terraces.*

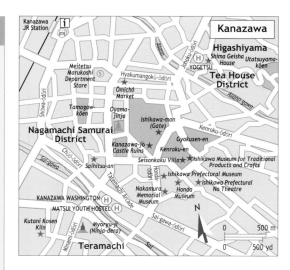

Kanazawa

Kanazawa JR Station · Meitetsu Marukoshi Department Store · Hyakumangokū-ōdōri · Ōmichō Market · Tamagaw-kōen · Oyama-jinja · Nagamachi Samurai District · Kanazawa-jō Castle Ruins · Saigawa · Chūō-dōri · Saihitsu-an · KANAZAWA WASHINGTON · MATSUI YOUTH HOSTEL · Kutani Kosen Kiln · Minami-ōdōri · Myōryū-ji (Ninja-dera) · **Teramachi** · Sai · *Higashiyama* · Shima Geisha House · Utatsuyama-kōen · YOGETSU · **Tea House District** · Asano-sawa · Ishikawa-mon (Gate) · Kenroku-ōdōri · Gyokusen-en · Kenroku-en · Seisonkaku Villa · Ishikawa Museum for Traditional Products and Crafts · Honda-dōri · Ishikawa Prefectural Museum · Ishikawa Prefectural Nō Theatre · Nakamura Memorial Museum · Honda Museum · Sai-gawa-ōdōri · N · 0   500 m · 0   500 yd

Seisonkaku ★★★

At the end of the Edo Period, the Maeda family was not about to give up its opulent lifestyle for Commodore Perry or anyone else. In 1863, adjoining Kenroku-en, the 13th Maeda lord built **Seisonkaku** as a villa for his mother. The formal *tatami* (traditional rice-straw matting) chambers downstairs, framed by magnificent carved beams, impart a sense of grandeur.

The upstairs decor is in the typically informal *shoin* style, featuring the study and bay window arrangement that became standard in samurai houses after the 15th century. The decor is sensationally Kaga-esque: ultramarine blue and ochre, with even the flamboyant touch of a 19th-century panel of Dutch glass in the paper window.

Around Kenroku-en ★★

The **Ishikawa Museum for Traditional Products and Crafts** near Seisonkaku is well worth visiting for an overview of Kaga crafts. It is open 09:00–17:00, closed every third Thur, Apr–Nov; every Thu, Dec–Mar.

Ishikawa-mon (gate) is the only part of Kanazawa Castle remaining from the 18th century; the sweep of the old outer walls still gives some idea of the complex's former scale. This part of town has been further enhanced by the restoration of some original features behind the gate.

Temples and Pleasure Quarters ★★★

Kanazawa has three main pockets of the past. **Nagamachi** is an area of sunny yellow, walled samurai houses that is much less self-consciously cultivated than Kurashiki's Bikan district. In Nagamachi there is an opportunity to see silk-dying at the **Saihitsu-an** (closed Thursdays), though explanations are in Japanese.

The **Teramachi** quarter west of the Sai River has 70 temples, of which the most famous is the **Myōryū-ji**, or Ninja Temple, known for its myriad passages and doors (visitors to the temple are required to join a guided tour). Across the Asano River it is well worth visiting the quiet streets of the **Higashiyama** district, where the 19th-century **Shima Geisha House** displays the same sort of daring decor as Seisonkaku. Open 09:00–18:00, admission ¥400.

Noto Peninsula ★★★

Noto is the Cape Cod of Japan; here, fishing and seaweed harvesting are still a way of life. **Wajima**, the main port, holds a bustling market every morning from 08:00–11:00 (except on the 10th and 25th of each month) and another one in the late afternoon, from 15:00 until sunset. At night, the lights of boats fishing for squid twinkle in the bay. The area has 813 laquerware workshops employing almost 3000 people. Visit the **Wajima Laquerware Centre**, open 08:00–17:00, Monday to Saturday.

The peninsula's main attraction is the remarkable **Senmaida** (thousand rice paddies) zig-zagging in terraces down to the sea along the rugged Sosogi coastline north of Wajima. On the beach by Nafune-Hakusan Shrine, the spectacular Gojinjo Daiko drumming festival is held from 31 July to 1 August.

KAGA CUISINE

Kanazawa is famous for Kaga cuisine. Kaga-style *kaiseki-ryōri* features various delicacies such as steamed lotus, tiny river fish called *gori*, and *jibu-ni* – a kind of stew made with duck. *Kabura-zushi*, made from yellowtail and turnips pickled in sake lees, tastes much better than it sounds. Winter cooking bursts with oysters and crab bought from the Ōmichō market. The people of Kaga are also known for their beautiful confectionery: one sweet, the *fuku-ume*, shaped like a plum blossom, is eaten at New Year.

Central Honshū at a Glance

Central Japan has some of the most **popular resorts** in the country. Avoid weekends, public holidays and in particular July–August, (peak season in the Japan Alps) although camping is always an option. Noto Peninsula too can get crowded in summer. **Spring** and **autumn** are pleasant everywhere, but book well in advance. The Nagano **skiing** season runs from late November to May.

Fuji-Hakone-Izu

For Hakone take the Odakyū line from Shinjuku to Hakone Yumoto. Buying a **Hakone Free Pass** (three days) or a **Hakone Weekday Pass** (two days, not valid at certain peak holiday times) gives unlimited use of transport. For Izu: go either by **JR** from Tokyo to Atami or by Odoriko Express direct to Shuzenji/Shimoda (JR pass holders pay extra, south of Itō).

Japan Alps

For the major gateways, take the Hokuriku **Shinkansen** from Tokyo to Nagano City or travel by **JR** from Shinjuku to Matsumoto. JR runs a service to Bessho Onsen from Tokyo via Ueda. Tsumago and Magome can be reached by JR either from Matsumoto or Nagoya. For Takayama either **fly** to Toyama, or go by JR from Nagoya. There is a bus service that runs from Tokyo to the slopes in peak skiing season.

Kanazawa

For Kanazawa take JR from Tokyo, Nagoya or Kyoto. Eiheiji is near Fukui on the JR line between Kyoto and Kanazawa.

Train and **bus** are adequate for side trips from Nagano (to Obuse and Togakushi) and from Matsumoto (Tsumago and Magome) or from Nagoya (to Inuyama and Meiji Mura). However, **hiring a car** in Atami makes sense for the Izu Peninsula (never ever contemplate driving from Tokyo) and in Kanazawa for the Noto Peninsula. Private vehicles are banned in Kamikōchi. Hiring a bicycle can be useful in Kanazawa and Takayama.

For budget *ryokan* and *minshuku*, try **JNTO's Welcome Inn** reservation service. For pension-style ski accommodation (including Nozawa Onsen) *see* www.snowjapan.com Price categories for *ryokan* and *minshuku* include, as a rule, two meals.

Fuji-Hakone-Izu
LUXURY

Yumoto Fujiya Hotel, 256-1 Yumoto, tel: 0460 5 6111, www.yumotofujiya.jp Opposite the original Fujiya.

BUDGET

Fuji-Hakone Guest House, 912 Sengokuhara Hakone

Kanagawa 250-0631, tel: 0460 84 6577, www.fujihakone.com Clean and very friendly. Natural hot spring.

K's House Mount Fuji, 6713-108, Funatsu, Fujikawaguchiko Minamitsuru-gu http://kshouse.jp/fuji-e/index.html Popular and friendly with good access to walking routes for Mount Fuji.

Izu Peninsula
MID-RANGE

Pension Sakuraya, 2584-20 Shirahama, Shimoda City, tel: 0558 23 4470, www.izu-sakuraya.jp/english A short walk from the beach. Inexpensive, good for families.

Japan Alps
LUXURY

Kamikōchi Imperial Hotel, Azumi-mura, Minami Azumi-gun, Nagano Prefecture, tel: 0263 95 2001, www.imperialhotel.co.jp/e This hotel boasts rustic opulence and a number of restaurants and bars.

MID-RANGE

Ryokan Fujioto, Tsumago Nagiso-machi, tel: 0264 57 30 09. Beautifully preserved 100-year-old *minshuku*, set amid a gorgeous Japanese garden.

BUDGET

Tokushawa Lodge, Kamikōchi, tel: 0263 95 2526. Right in the heart of the best walking district, you can make the most of the 'Yosemite of Japan' from this simple, practical base.

Central Honshū at a Glance

Bessho Onsen
MID-RANGE
Hanaya Bessho Onsen,
169 Bessho Onsen, Ueda
City, tel: 0268 38 3131.
Possibly the finest *ryokan* in
this historical area.
Chōju-kan, Hōshi Onsen,
Nagai, Niihari-mura, Tone-
gun, Gunma Prefecture, tel:
0278 55 0055. Famous, atmospheric old wooden bathhouse.

Kanazawa
MID-RANGE
Kanazawa Washington Hotel,
1-10-18 Katamachi, Kanazawa
City, tel: 076 224 0111. Close
to Kenroku-en. Chinese and
Japanese restaurants.

BUDGET
Yogetsu, 1-13-22,
Higashiyama, Kanazawa 920-
0831, tel: 076 252 049.
100-year-old *minshuku*, well
located in the traditional
geisha district.

Noto
BUDGET
Minshuku Hegura, 91
Kamimachi, Fugeshimachi,
Wajima City, tel: 0768 22
1018. Charming old wooden
house in good location. Near
the Sumiyoshi Shrine.

Fuji-Hakone-Izu
Best for food is Lake
Yamanaka, where there are
lots of restaurants, many
concentrated around the
waterfront in Asahigaoka.

Japan Alps
Most pension and Japanese-
style accommodation include
two meals.
Nagano
A large number of good restaurants on Chūō-dōri towards
Zenkō-ji. Various price ranges.
Matsumoto
Mikawaya, Chūō 3, tel: 0263
32 0339. *The* place to try
horsemeat (*ba-sashi* and
sakura-nabe).
Takayama
Selection of bars and cafés. A
vegetarian's paradise, famous
for its soba noodles. Another
local speciality is *hoba-miso* –
vegetables mixed with miso,
wrapped in a magnolia tree leaf
and roasted over an open flame.
Kanazawa
The best value seafood is
around the market. There are
restaurants in the Kōrinbō 109
Building (Katamachi), and in
hotels such as the Washington.
Kotobukiya, 2-14-13
Owaricho, tel: 076 231 6245.
Shojin-ryōri in a magnificent
Kaga mansion setting. Reservations essential. Expensive.

Japan Travel Bureau, tel: 03
5796 5454, for Sunrise Tours
with English-speaking guide
to Mount Fuji-Hakone.

Fuji-Hakone-Izu
JNTO TIC in Tokyo has plenty
of information on this area.
Nissan Rent-a-car (a three-
minute walk from Atami
Station), tel: 0120 00 4123.
Nagano
Tourist Information Centre
(Nagano Station), tel: 026 226
5626. Maps, information,
bookings. Open 09:00–18:00.
Matsumoto
Tourist Information Centre
(by Matsumoto Station), tel: 026
332 2814. Open 09:30–18:00.
Nagoya
Tourist Information Centre
(Nagoya Station), tel: 052 541
4301. Open 09:00–19:00.
Kanazawa
Tourist Information Centre
(Kanazawa Station), tel: 076
232 6200. Also has a
Goodwill Guide Service desk.
Nippon Rent-a-Car (near
Kanazawa Station), tel: 076
263 0919.
**Ishikawa Foundation for
International Exchange**,
Rifare Building, 3F, 1-5-3
Hon-machi, Kanazawa, tel:
076 262 5931, www.ifie.or.
jp/english/facilities/center/
index.html Library stocks a
large number of foreign pub-
lications, aimed principally
at foreign residents.

KANAZAWA	J	F	M	A	M	J	J	A	S	O	N	D
AVERAGE TEMP. °C	3	3	6	12	17	21	25	27	22	16	11	6
AVERAGE TEMP. °F	37	37	43	54	63	70	77	80	72	61	52	43
RAINFALL mm	293	195	157	148	150	207	251	171	248	203	265	305
RAINFALL in	11.5	7.7	6.2	5.8	5.9	8.2	9.9	6.7	9.8	8.0	10.4	12.0
DAYS OF RAINFALL	25	21	11	14	8	14	10	10	12	13	19	24

5
Kyoto and Kinki

The Kinki region is the **heartland of old Japan** where the first capital of **Yamato** was established and where the emperors languished in Kyoto after their glory days during the Heian Period. Even today, the crafts, arts and festivals of Kyoto and Nara still have an aristocratic air – unlike Ōsaka, which is much more commercial and down to earth.

Do not despair, as you pull into Kyoto Station's cavernous steel-and-glass Star Wars structure, that the genteel world of *The Tale of Genji* is entirely lost; is simply hiding under layers of urban accretion. In fact, Kyoto's wealth of 1600 temples, 270 shrines, 200 gardens and 500 festivals is so mind-boggling that any visitor to the city runs the risk of premature burn-out. To avoid this, concentrate on very few sites at a time and do not be afraid to wander off into nooks and crannies not mentioned in the guidebooks.

In comparison with Kyoto, Nara is less mentally and physically demanding. **The Great Buddha of Tōdai-ji** welcomes you with an enigmatic smile and the rest more or less takes care of itself. It is always worth timing a visit to Nara to take place in autumn in order to catch the annual exhibition of **Shōsō-in treasures** at the **National Museum,** which affords a privileged peep into the world's oldest imperial chest of drawers.

The place that wraps the layers of history up again is **Kōya-san**, one of Japan's great temple sites. In the vast, shady Okuno-in necropolis, the ashes of the great and the obscure have mingled for 11 centuries.

DON'T MISS

★★★ **Higashiyama:** Ginkaku-ji and Kiyomizu-dera's magic.
★★★ **Hanami-kōji and Ponto-chō:** old geisha quarters, Kyoto.
★★★ **Sanjūsangen-dō:** 1001 gilded images of Kannon.
★★★ **Byōdō-in:** 'Phoenix Hall' from days of *The Tale of Genji.*
★★★ **Great Buddha of Tōdai-ji:** the essence of Nara.
★★★ **Hōryū-ji:** Buddhist art.
★★★ **Kōya-san:** temples galore and Okuno-in necropolis.
★★★ **Himeji Castle:** a soaring symbol of feudal Japan.
★★ **Ōsaka Aquarium:** marine life from the Pacific Ring of Fire.

Opposite: *The waters of Kiyomizu-dera are said to cure all ills.*

CLIMATE

The Kinki region is as hot as the Kantō region in summer, if not hotter. (Ōsaka is marginally warmer than Kyoto.) June, July and September are the wettest months. The cherry blossom season starts in late March and the autumn leaves start to change colour in mid-October. In December the minimum temperature sinks to around 2ºC (36ºF), but there is little rainfall and plenty of sunny days.

KYOTO

Kyoto is navigation-friendly thanks to its **grid pattern**. Numbered avenues running east–west, such as Shijō-dōri (Fourth Avenue), intersect with major streets running north–south. As a rule, all temples and shrines are open daily, but admission times and charges vary.

The central area around the station, Nijō Castle and the Imperial Palace is very much **Establishment Kyoto**. Night life focuses on **Ponto-chō** and Kiyamachi west of the Kamo River and, on the east bank, in **Gion**. **Arashiyama** in the west is a favourite for autumn colours. The grandest Zen temples are found in the northwest. **Higashiyama** in the east is more immediately inviting and easily covered on foot.

Before buying anything, the best place to gain an understanding of the huge variety of Kyoto crafts is the **Fureaikan** (Kyoto Museum of Traditional Crafts) and the Kyoto Handicraft Centre near Heian-jingū (*see* At a Glance, page 97).

Takashimaya department store at the corner of Kawaramachi-dōri and Shijō-dōri is the main shopping area. On Kawaramachi there is also a Maruzen bookstore and Yamato Mingei-ten (folk crafts). The **Kiyomizu** area is excellent for pottery. Teramachi-dōri and the arcades north of Shijō-dōri are worth a browse, but try to visit one of the **flea markets** at Tō-ji (1st Sunday and 21st of the month) or at Kitano Tenman-gū (25th of the month). Parallel with Shijō-dōri, is Kyoto's old food market.

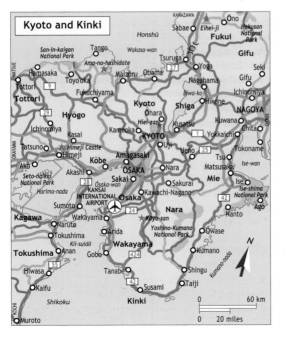

Nijō Castle ★★★

Nijō-jō (castle) was the private Kyoto residence of the Tokugawa *shōguns*. It is one of Kyoto's many UNESCO World Heritage sites. Construction started under Ieyasu in 1602 and lasted for over 20 years. However, as the 17th century progressed very few

shōguns bothered coming to Kyoto; the castle simply became a status symbol to remind the imperial family who really ruled Japan. The *donjon* burned down in 1750 and was never rebuilt.

Above: *The imposing walls of Nijō Castle testify to its militaristic origins.*

Today, the star attraction is the **Ni-no-maru Palace**. This comprises five chambers linked by corridors complete with squeaky 'nightingale' floors to alert against intruders. Artists of the **Kanō School** went berserk on the interiors: the outer chamber, for low-ranking visitors, is decorated with images of tigers and leopards; the interior of the *Ōhiroma* (Grand Chamber), where the *shōgun* received guests on a dais, is heavy on hawks and pine trees. Like Himeji, Nijō is a statement of tasteful dictatorship. Open 08:45–17:00. Admission ¥600.

Arashiyama ★★

The blossoms of Arashiyama are the soul of Japanese literature, epitomizing the impermanence of all things – except tourism. In November, thousands come to view the **Momiji** (maple leaves). One way of appreciating the scenery is to take the Torokko train from Arashiyama to Kameoka and float the 16km (10 miles) back down the Hozu River by boat.

Arashiyama is also a good place to walk or cycle along bamboo-lined lanes. The biggest draw is **Tenryū-ji**, a Rinzai-sect temple. The complex is now a shadow of its former self, but the garden and pond are a subtle blend of Heian and Zen design well worth seeing. Open 08:30–17:30 (until 17:00, November–March).

FROM TEA CEREMONY TO IKEBANA

The **Urasenke Foundation** offers a range of courses on the tea ceremony and holds weekly demonstrations, *see* www.urasenke.org
The **Kyoto Handicraft Centre** has a 'Handicraft School' that allows you to have a go at woodblock printing, doll making or cloisonné. *See* http://kyotoguide.com for information about *ikebana*, *origami* as well as Japanese cooking and language classes.
The **Gion Corner** show (Yasaka Kaikan at the south end of Hanami-kōji) holds nightly performances of traditional music and dancing from March–November. For information on performing arts, check the monthly Kyoto Visitors' Guide, www.kyotoguide.com

Above: *The golden façade of Kinkaku-ji.*

CULTURAL EVENTS

• 1–30 April: **Miyako Odori** (Cherry Dance) at Gion Kaburenjo. Annual dance by Gion *maiko* and *geisha*.
• 15 May: **Aoi Matsuri** (Hollyhock Festival) held at the Kamagamo and Shimogamo shrines.
• 1–2 June: **Takigi-Nō** (Torchlight Nō) at Heian Jingū.
• July: **Gion Matsuri**, one of Japan's top three festivals.
• 16 August: **Daimonji Festival**, when bonfires, including two in the shape of the *kanji* for *dai* (big) are lit on the hills around Kyoto.
• 22 October: **Jidai Matsuri** (Festival of the Ages). A huge costumed parade from the Imperial Palace to Heian Jingū.

Kinkaku-ji (Temple of the Golden Pavilion) ★★

In 1397 **Ashikaga Yoshimitsu** (1358–1408) retired to an estate in northwest Kyoto, marked by the Golden Pavilion remaining today. In 1950 the Pavilion was burned to the ground by a psychopathically jealous monk, whose story is fictionalized in Mishima Yukio's *The Golden Pavilion*. The present reconstruction is covered in a staggering 20kg (44 pounds) of gold leaf. It is the most attractively Chinese of Kyoto's temples, yet its soul was somehow consumed in the flames 50 years ago.

The architecture of Kinkaku-ji was startlingly novel in Yoshimitsu's time, combining the formal style of an imperial hall downstairs with elements taken from a **samurai** residence on the middle floor and a Zen meditation room on the top floor featuring a cusp-arched window and panelled doors. Open 09:00–17:00.

Ryōan-ji ★★★

The garden of this famous Zen temple is an aesthetic institution. Dating from around 1500, it comprises 15 boulders grouped in a raked bed of gravel. To enter into the Zen spirit, the idea is to contemplate whether the shapes represent islands in the ocean, mountain tops above clouds, or oneness with infinity. It is open 08:00–17:00, March–November; 08:30–16:30, December–February.

Saihō-ji ★★★

The garden of Saihō-ji, or Koke-dera (Moss Temple) is the antithesis to the barren austerity of Ryōan-ji, though Zen in inspiration. It is uncertain what remains of Musō Soseki's landscaping from 1339. Over the centuries, however, this two-tier garden has grown into a veritable magic carpet of crushed velvet spangled with countless varieties and shades of moss. To see this astonishing spectacle you must apply to the temple at least three weeks in advance, pay a hefty fee and participate in a Zen service (ask JNTO for details). If this is simply not feasible, other 'moss' opportunities include the garden at **Rokuō-in** in Arashiyama and the north garden at **Ryōgen-in** in Daitoku-ji.

Sanjūsangen-dō (Thirty-three Bay Hall) ★★★

Rengeō-in, as this temple is officially known, is an extraordinary sight. The present building dates from 1266. Inside, an army of **1001 images of Kannon** (goddess of mercy) stand ranged in silent splendour, ready to save the world from *mappō* (terminal decline); multiplied by 33 (the number of Kannon's manifestations), the troops actually number 33,033. Seventy master craftsmen took 100 years to achieve this result. In mid-January an archery contest is held outdoors along the length of the 118m (387ft) verandah. Open 08:00–17:00, March–October; 09:00–16:00, November–February.

Kyoto National Museum ★★

Kyoto's main museum covers all aspects of the city's culture and history and has dozens of national treasures. A new Collections Hall is being built, due to open in 2013. *See* www.kyohaku.go.jp for exhibition details.

Gion and Ponto-chō ★★★

On either side of the Kamo River lie the traditional *geisha* quarters of Kyoto. Ponto-chō, parallel with the river on the west, is quite magical by night, a lantern-lit alleyway that houses some exceedingly exclusive and expensive bars, as well as more reasonable restaurants.

On the surface, Gion is the bigger, flashier night spot, although the back streets are more intimate. **Hanami-kōji**, a narrow lane dating from the 17th century, is still prime *geisha* territory; here behind ochre-coloured walls is **Ichiriki-tei**, Kyoto's single most famous teahouse. This is a perfect area for wandering around on foot. The Shirakawa Area, by the Shirakawa Canal, is the quietest part, and very beautiful.

IMPERIAL VILLAS

Kyoto has two exquisite 17th-century imperial villas, as well as the Imperial Palace (which is rather staid and lifeless). Katsura Rikyū (Imperial Villa) in southwest Kyoto has a magnificent garden dotted with teahouses. The villa buildings, in classical **sukiya style**, are light and simple, a complete contrast to the ornate style of Nijō Castle. Shūgaku-in Rikyū (northeast Kyoto) is a series of three villas built by Emperor Go-mizuno'o (r.1611–29) in expansive grounds at the foot of Hiei-zan. Visits to all Kyoto's imperial residences must be made **by appointment** with the Imperial Household Agency. Apply online at http://sankan.kunai cho.go.jp/english/index.html

Below: *A carpet of moss covers the ground at Ryōgen-in, Daitoku-ji.*

Below: *The dazzling façade of Heian Jingū, built in early Heian Period style.*

Heian Jingū ★★

This blaze of vermilion and white with green-tiled roofs is dedicated to Emperor Kammu, the first emperor of Heian-kyō, and Emperor Kōmei (r.1846–67), the last emperor. Built in 1895, it is modelled on the **Daigoku-den** (Hall of State) of Heian-kyō's first imperial palace; it is, therefore, a good approximation of early Heian Period architecture, when Chinese influence was still significant. The Heian-style gar-dens behind are particularly attractive at cherry-blossom time in spring. Open 08:30–17:30, March–August; 08:30–17:00, September–October and 1–14 May; 08:30–16:30, the rest of the year.

Kiyomizu-dera (Pure Water Temple) ★★★

Follow the hordes of navy-uniformed school children up the slopes of Kiyomizu-zaka, Sannen-zaka or Ninnen-zaka, past pottery and pickle shops, and you cannot miss Kiyomizu-dera. The present building, perched on **wooden stilts** above Kyoto, dates from 1633, though Kiyomizu has been a temple site since AD778.

The temple was founded on the site of the Otawa water-fall (its name refers to the clarity and purity of the water) and you can still drink from three steams that flow at the temple. You get beautiful views over the city from the wooden platform, and the Jishu Shrine inside is dedicated to the god of love and matchmaking. Open 06:00–dusk.

Ginkaku-ji (Temple of the Silver Pavilion) ★★★

As a matter of fact, the strikingly plain pavilion of Ashikaga Yoshimasa is no more silver than the Blue Mosque in Istanbul is blue. Ginkaku-ji took some 30 years to build. By the time Yoshimasa retired here in 1482, plans to cover the exterior in silver leaf had evaporated; now the only glimpse of 'silver' is an assiduously raked sea of sand surrounding a truncated sand cone, probably introduced some time in the early 17th century as a moon-viewing device. In Yoshimasa's day, Ginkaku-ji epitomized the so-called Higashiyama style of Zen understatement. It is open 08:30–17:00, March–November; 09:00–17:00, December–February.

AROUND KYOTO

Ama-no-hashidate (Bridge to Heaven), on the Sea of Japan coast in northern Kyoto Prefecture, is a narrow 3.5km (2.2-mile) sand spit across Miyazu Bay. **Hiei-zan**, situated just northeast of Kyoto, is the headquarters of the

Tendai sect, founded in AD805 by Saichō (known posthumously as Dengyō Daishi).

Ama-no-hashidate ★★

Like Miyajima and Matsushima, Ama-no-hashidate is one of Japan's top scenic spots. Ama-no-hashidate is supposedly best viewed upside down from Kasamatsu Park, by standing with the head between the legs in order to make the sand spit look as if it is floating in the air; it is actually far more rewarding to take the 60-minute walk to the end of the spit among the kind of wind-battered pine trees that inspired the art of **bonsai**.

Kompon Chū-dō of Enryaku-ji (Hiei-zan) ★★★

The institution on this heavily forested ridge was once immensely powerful; it even had its own army. In 1571, however, Ōda Nobunaga took exception to the monks' anarchical tendencies and laid waste to the entire complex. Most of the 100 or so buildings present today date from the 17th century. Enryaku-ji, Hiei-zan's

---

TETSUGAKU NO MICHI (THE PHILOSOPHER'S WALK)

Nishida Kitarō (1870–1945), modern Japan's most important philosopher, walked the 2km (1.3-mile) path along the Shishigatani Canal in northeast Kyoto every morning. Although Kyoto has many walking opportunities, this one, from just north of **Nanzen-ji** to **Ginkaku-ji**, is good for getting away from it all. En route are two small temples called Anraku-ji and Hōnen-in. Hōnen-in is open only in the first week of April and November, but is well worth visiting for its Momoyama screens. There are also several coffee shops along the canal.

Right: *The splendour of 17th-century Ming China can still be appreciated today at Mampuku-ji.*

---

main temple, has two compounds. The **Kompon Chū-dō** of the Tō-tō (Eastern Compound) has one of the most breathtakingly mysterious interiors of any temple in Japan, thick with the aroma of incense and cedar wood – almost more Tibetan than Japanese. The dimly lit sunken inner sanctum, occupied by the *Yakushi* (Buddha of Medicine) and his attendants, is a haven of peace. The Shaka-dō (Buddha Hall) of the Sai-tō (Western Compound) echoes the Kompon Chū-dō, but not nearly as resolutely. Open 08:30–16:30, March–November; 08:30–16:00, December–February.

Ōhara ★★

The village of Ōhara beneath Hiei-zan is no longer quite as rustic as it was in the Heian Period, but there is still a suitably poignant atmosphere at Jakkō-in, the small nunnery where the Empress Kenrei-mon-in withdrew from the world after seeing her child, Antoku, drown at the Battle of Dan-no-ura in 1185. The nearby temple of Sanzen-in, is particularly famous for its autumn colours, and its Amida Buddha dating from AD985.

Mampuku-ji ★★

Mampuku-ji, the headquarters of the Zen Ōbaku sect, was established near Uji in 1661. Mampuku-ji receives many fewer visitors than Byōdō-in, its much more famous and quintessentially Japanese neighbour at Uji. Yet it provides a spacious, exotic antithesis of Ming-style Zen architecture and raked sand. The name Ōbaku refers to the Chinese cork trees in the vicinity. Uji is also well known for its tea.

Byōdō-in ★★★

The Byōdō-in was the private villa of Fujiwara Michinaga. In 1052, Michinaga's son converted it into a temple. The breathtaking **Hoō-dō** (Phoenix Hall) was completed in 1053, when the world was thought to be on the verge of *mappō* (*see* page 25) and only Amida could provide popular salvation. The Phoenix Hall and pond represent an architectural recreation of Amida's Western Paradise.

The name 'phoenix' originates from the two graceful wings flanking the central hall. Inside, the imposing image of Amida is the only authenticated work of the sculptor **Jōchō**. Also the work of Jōchō and his school are a series of 52 playful little bodhisattvas, all dancers and musicians riding the clouds. The new **Byōdō-in Museum**, completed in 2001, now provides better viewing of the Phoenix Hall treasures, including some of the Bodhisattvas, which take on new dimensions at eye level. Open 08:30–17:30, admission ¥600.

NARA AND BEYOND

Nara is laid out on a grid system in the same way as Kyoto. The majority of the central sights are clustered in and around Nara Park (which is populated by over 1000 deer) and the pond of Sarusawa-ike. The most

MIHO MUSEUM

The Miho Museum (www. miho.or.jp/english/index.htm) in the Shiga mountains southeast of Kyoto is an architectural triumph of geo-metrical glass roofs among tree tops. Designed by IM Pei for the Shūmeikai, a wealthy religious sect, it cost US$216 million to build. The North Wing is devoted to Chinese and Japanese art, and the South Wing to Egyptian, Greek, Roman and Islamic works of **world-class quality**. The collection also has stunning Gandharan Buddhist sculptures. The Miho Museum is at 300 Momodani, Shigaraki-chō, Koga-gun, Shiga Prefecture, tel: 0748 82 3411. Open 10:00–17:00, Tuesday–Sunday, 16 March to 10 June, 1 July to 22 August and 1 September to 15 December. Admission ¥1000. Take the JR Tōkaidō line from Kyoto to JR Ishiyama Station then change to Teisan bus.

Left: *The Miho Museum, one of Japan's best-kept secrets, houses an extensive collection of Japanese and inter-national art.*

logical route from either the Kintetsu or JR station is down Sanjō-dōri, past the Nara City Tourist Information Office, and on to Kōfuku-ji, immediately recognizable by its Five-storeyed Pagoda.

Kōfuku-ji ★★★

Kōfuku-ji is the ancestral temple of the **Fujiwara family**. Established in Nara in AD710, it originally consisted of 175 buildings. Today only six remain, all of them rebuilt between the 12th and 15th centuries. On sunny days, reflections of the Five-storeyed Pagoda as well as its smaller three-storeyed neighbour ripple across the surface of Sarusawa-ike.

Both the Tōkon-dō (the East Golden Hall), which dates back to the early 15th century, and the modern Kokuhō-kan (the National Treasure Hall) contain numerous masterpieces of Buddhist sculpture, including a 7th-century **Yakushi bronze head**. Both halls are open 09:00–17:00.

Tōdai-ji ★★★

Tōdai-ji was founded in AD745 by the Emperor Shōmu. As a symbol of the power of Buddhism and the imperial throne, it oozes the very essence of the Nara Period.

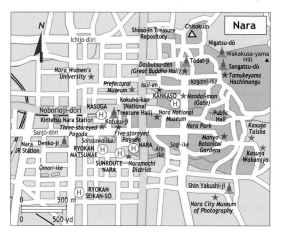

The Great Buddha, an image of Vairocana, or the **Cosmic Buddha**, was consecrated in AD752, making him 500 years older than the one in Kamakura. At 15m (49ft), he is also 3.3m (11ft) taller. He has, however, fared less well over the centuries, losing his head twice; his upper torso and head were last recast in 1692. The present **Daibutsu-den** (Great Buddha Hall) of 1709 is much smaller than the

Left: *Priests invoking kami at the Kasuga Taisha, shrine of the Fujiwara family.*

original. Even so, at 57m (187ft) wide, 49m (161ft) high and 50.4m (165ft) deep, it is the largest wooden building in the world. Open daily, 07:30–17:30 (08:00 from November–March, 16:30 from November through February and 17:00 in March and October).

The other wonder of Tōdai-ji is the **Shōsō-in**, an 8th-century log storehouse, which for centuries safeguarded the greatest inventoried collection of 7th- and 8th-century oriental and Central Asian treasures anywhere in the world. The collection contains 9000 items.

Each year from late October to early November, the **Nara National Museum** stages an annual two-week exhibition of **Shōsō-in treasures**. The objects on show range from musical instruments to exquisite textiles and jewellery, all in immaculate condition. During the rest of the year, the museum displays items from its permanent collections of Asuka and Nara Period art. Open 09:30–17:00, Tuesday–Sunday and until 19:00 on Fridays during summer, admission ¥500. *See* www.narahaku.go.jp

MAIN FESTIVALS

• 15 January: **Yama-yaki** (Grass-burning Festival). At 18:00 priests from Kōfuku-ji set fire to the grass on Wakakusa-yama, supposedly re-enacting a border dispute with the monks of Tōfuku-ji.
• 1–14 March: **O-taimatsu** and **O-mizutori** (Torch-lighting and Water-drawing Festival). The culmination of two weeks of rites by the monks of Tōdai-ji at Nigatsu-dō opposite the Daibutsu-den. Embers from the torches are scattered to ward off evil spirits and water from the well is offered to the Eleven-headed Kannon.
• 11–12 May: **Takigi-Nō** (Torch-lit Nō) at Kōfuku-ji and Kasuga Shrine.
• 15–18 December: **On-matsuri**, a costumed procession at the Kasuga Shrine with dance and Nō performances.

Above: *Children on a school outing feed one of the many deer in Nara Park.*

Kasuga Taisha ★★

A long lantern-lined path leads up to this
attractive vermilion shrine dedicated to the
Fujiwara family. Like the Ise shrines, the
main structure is rebuilt every 20 years, but
remains faithful to the original 8th-century
architecture. According to legend, the four
kami enshrined here were carried to Nara by
the deer whose descendents still graze here
today. Kasuga is a prime venue for festivals
and **dance performances**. It is open 06:30–
17:30, admission ¥500 to enter inner shrine.

Shin Yakushi-ji ★★★

This temple is refreshingly simple. Dedicated
to **Yakushi** (Buddha of Medicine), it was founded in
AD747 by Empress Kōmyō. The building is the oldest,
unadulterated temple building within Nara and a designated **National Treasure**. So is the central image of the
Buddha himself, a startling figure carved out of one block
of wood, not to mention his **Twelve Divine Generals**, all
posturing in clay. If you can cope with only one dose of
Nara sculpture, take it from the Buddha of Medicine; the
sense of intimacy and authenticity at Shin Yakushi-ji is
unparalleled. Open 09:00–17:00, daily, admission ¥300.

Nara City Museum of Photography ★★

This modern temple-style structure next door to Shin
Yakushi-ji opened in 1992. It houses 80,000 images by
Irie Taikichi, a photographer who devoted his life to the
landscapes and Buddhist images of old Yamato. The
Taishō Period collection of Kudo Risaburo offers nostalgic
glimpses of Nara in the days when Hōryū-ji was still out
in the fields. Exhibitions are on a rotating basis. Open
09:30–17:00, Tuesday–Sunday. *See* www.dnp.co.jp/
museum/nara/nara-e.html

Hōryū-ji ★★★

Hōryū-ji, southwest of Nara, is Japan's most remarkable
temple site both for its age and quality of architecture

and objects, many of which are on permanent display in the **Tokyo National Museum** (*see* page 34). Traditionally dated to AD607, a temple known as Wakakusa-dera was founded on this site in the time of **Crown Prince Shōtoku**. After it burned down in AD670 it was replaced by the Hōryū-ji complex that remains today. This comprises a remarkable mix of original buildings and 10th- to 14th-century reconstructions, enhanced throughout a 20-year period of restoration from 1933–53.

The complex is divided into the **Sai-in Garan** (Western Precinct) and the **Tō-in** (Eastern Precinct) separated by the **Daihōzō-den** (Treasure Hall). The star attractions of the Sai-in are the **Five-storeyed Pagoda**, dating from AD693, and the slightly earlier **Kon-dō** (Golden Hall), which is the oldest wooden building in the world. Inside, canopies hang above a central Shaka (historical Buddha) and boddhisattvas. The original murals were largely destroyed by fire in 1949; apart from a few fragments, today's paintings are reproductions.

The Treasure Hall contains numerous Buddhist statues as well as images of Prince Shōtoku. Its most famous item, however, is the **Tamamushi** (Jewel Beetle) Shrine, which dates from circa AD650. The Tō-in is dominated by the striking octagonal **Yume-dono** (Dream Hall); nearby is the small nunnery of Chūgū-ji, which was originally the residence of Shōtoku's mother, and another Treasure Hall. Open 08:00–16:30. *See* www.horyuji.or.jp/horyuji_e.htm

Ise ★

Ise is the home of Amaterasu, the sun goddess. The **Naikū** (Inner Shrine), established in the 4th century, houses Amaterasu's mirror (one of the three sacred imperial regalia). The **Gekū** (Outer Shrine), 6km (3.7 miles) away, is dedicated to the kami of food. Though the shrine grounds are atmo-

THE AGE OF FOREIGN INFLUENCE

The Asuka and Nara periods were characterized by foreign influence, unlike the Heian Period, when Japan began to turn to itself and create its own art and literature. The temple of Tōshōdai-ji west of Nara, founded by the Chinese monk Ganjin in 759, is built with all the stateliness of Tang Dynasty China. At Hōryū-ji, the cloud corbels carved in wooden beams and the drapes of the early 7th-century statuary bear strong Chinese influence. The intricate bronze filigree banners and canopies echo Korean and Central Asian examples.

Below: *The Five-storeyed Pagoda is one of Hōryū-ji's star attractions.*

spheric, the Naikū in particular flirts tantalizingly behind several layers of fencing, showing off only her roof and the odd beam. Mortals are not allowed to get any closer to Amaterasu's residence, which makes this a pleasant, but not entirely satisfying outing.

KŌYA-SAN

Kōya-san, founded by Kūkai (known posthumously as **Kōbō Daishi**) is a mass of temples, pagodas, shrines and souvenir shops all jostling for space on a ridge reached by funicular railway as well as the inevitable tour buses. It may all seem slightly disappointing at first, but spending a night here and listening to the sonorous chanting of morning prayers is one of the best experiences you can have in Japan.

Kongōbu-ji ★★★

This striking temple built by Toyotomi Hideyoshi in 1593 later became the headquarters of the Shingon sect. Although rebuilt in the 19th century, it still boasts late 16th-century panels of cranes and blossoms painted by the **Kano** school, whose works grace the greatest of all Momoyama and Edo Period edifices. Hideyoshi's nephew is said to have committed ritual suicide in front of the paintings in the **Yanagi-no-ma** (Willow Room).

The **Garan**, (Central Compound) is altogether less compelling. The site is dominated by the garish **Kompon Daitō**, the great stupa last rebuilt in the 1930s, and the Kon-dō, where Kūkai reputedly first lectured. The **Reihō-kan** (Treasure Hall) is dingy and badly labelled, but a must for anyone interested in Buddhist art. Open 08:30–17:00.

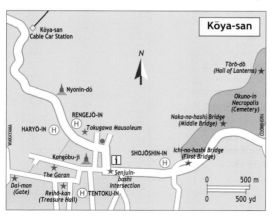

Left: *The art of Japanese gardening involves the harmonious blending of man-made elements (such as this bridge) with nature.*

Okuno-in ★★★

Kōya-san's real gem is Okuno-in, a moss-encrusted necropolis stretching 1.5km (1 mile) from the Ichi-no-hashi (First Bridge) to the flickering **Tōrō-dō** (**Hall of Lanterns**). Behind the hall is a small, simple mausoleum, where Kūkai is believed to sit in eternal meditation. Chief executives and school children alike come here to bow their heads in reverence.

Along the cool, pine-shaded path over half a million souls are commemorated by sleek, black marble slabs, crumbling stupas and, in one case, a model of a space rocket. This is the Who's Who of Japan's spirit world, where the ashes of generals, feudal lords and Toyota employees mingle with those of pacifists and priests. At dusk, lanterns light up this compelling land of ghosts. Open 06:00–17:30.

ŌSAKA

Like Tokyo, Ōsaka improves on closer inspection. Japan's commercial capital has solid people, good food and enough entertainment to provide a few diversions between business appointments or trains.

Near Umeda Station is the **Umeda Sky Building**, a pair of 40-storeyed towers joined at the top by a spectacular garden observatory suspended at 170m (558ft). The elevator ride is not cheap, but worth the weird

---

THE MONK KŪKAI (AD774–835)

As every Japanese school child knows, Kūkai was the *wunderkind* of Japanese civilization. Born at Zentsū-ji on Shikoku in 774, he travelled to China in 804 to study esoteric Buddhism. Not content with returning to Japan to found the Shingon sect on Kōya-san, he also became a master of Chinese poetry, painting, calligraphy and civil engineering. As a **scholar of Sanskrit**, he is also traditionally accredited with the invention of the *kana* script (whose syllabic structure bears some resemblance to Sanskrit).

Above: *Incense braziers line a temple verandah.*
Opposite: *The impressive soaring white ramparts of Himeji Castle.*

TENJIN FESTIVAL

The **Sannō Festival** of Asakusa, the **Gion Festival** in Kyoto and Osaka's **Tenjin Festival** at the Kitano-Tenman-gū are the top three in Japan. Held on 24–25 July, the Tenjin Festival dates from AD951, when purification rites were held to protect against infectious diseases at the height of summer. On the 24th, a child is rowed out into the river holding a halberd, which it hurls into the water. On the 25th the festival transfers to the river, where numerous boats sail into the evening to the sound of drumming, ancient Shinto music, dancing and fireworks.

---

sensation. Open 10:00–22:00. South of Ōsaka Station is the recently refurbished **Museum of Oriental Ceramics**, which has some of the finest Chinese and Korean ceramics in Japan. Open 09:30–17:00, admission ¥300. *See* www.moco.or.jp/en/index.html

A number of Ōsaka's great theatres for the traditional performing arts are in the Minami district around Namba Station. The **National Bunraku Theatre** has twice-daily performances of Bunraku during the months of January, April, June, August and November (English commentaries of the shows are available). *See* www.ntj.jac.go.jp/english/index.html

Fun Ōsaka ★★★

Tempozan Harbour Village is the site of the mammoth **Ōsaka Aquarium**. The star attraction is the whale shark, who lives in a central tank representing the Pacific Ocean. In a descending spiral around this tank are 15 other tanks housing sea otters, dolphins, penguins, crabs and even jellyfish from around the **Pacific Ring of Fire**. The scene of humans and marine life ogling each other is rather like a *Far Side* cartoon. Open 10:00–20:00, last admission 19:00. Expect to queue on weekends. *See* www.kaiyukan.com/index.html

Nearby attractions include a giant Ferris wheel, the Suntory Museum, an IMAX theatre and, on its own waterfront site, **Universal Studios theme park**: for tickets and access, *see* www.usj.co.jp/e_top.html

Ethnic Ōsaka ★★

Ōsaka is home to many *burakumin*. It is also home to the **Ōsaka Human Rights Museum**, better known as **Liberty Ōsaka**. Nowhere else in Japan will you learn more about taboo topics such as ethnic discrimination, women's rights and even environmental disasters. CD commentary is available in English and Korean. The museum reopened in December 2005 after refurbishment. Open 10:00–17:00, Tuesday–Sunday. *See* www.liberty.or.jp/topfile/human-top.htm

KŌBE AND BEYOND

First-time visitors would be hard pushed to know that Kōbe was devastated by an earthquake in 1995. The city's recovery – superficially at least – has been quite remarkable. As one of Japan's treaty ports, Kōbe has the same elements as Nagasaki and Yokohama: Chinatown is in the Nankin-machi area; the old foreigners' residential district (*ijin-kan*) is in Kitano, which also has a mosque, dating from 1935, and a Jain Temple.

Himeji Castle ★★★

One building that has most definitely shrugged off the 1995 earthquake – and numerous others over the past 400 years – is Himeji Castle, the pièce de résistance of all Japanese military architecture. Known as **Shirasagi-jō** (White Heron Castle) because of its soaring, white façade, Himeji was completed in 1609 for Tokugawa Ieyasu's son-in-law. It is the one fortification left in Japan that imparts a true sense of the new stability and prosperity ushered in by the Tokugawa *shōgunate* in the early 17th century.

Himeji's outer moat has long since disappeared but the inner moat, the maze of walls, watch towers, gates and the inner citadel – complete with 33m (108ft) *donjon* – are all original. To appreciate fully the architectural features, consider taking a tour with an English-speaking volunteer guide, although the route is reasonably self-explanatory. It is open 09:00–16:00, September–May; 09:00–17:00, June–August.

> ### YOSHINO-KUMANO NATIONAL PARK
>
> The Yoshino-Kumano National Park lies at the junction of Nara and Wakayama prefectures, south of Ōsaka. The Park contains the **three ancient shrines of Kumano**, Hongū, Shingū and Nachi, whose kami supposedly came to the aid of the mythical Emperor Jimmu. At Nachi there is also the Nachi Falls, one of Japan's most spectacular cascades, which tumbles over a cliff face from a height of 133m (436ft). The temple at Nachi is the starting point of a 33-Kannon-Temple pilgrimage that ends north of Lake Biwa.

Kyoto and Kinki at a Glance

Spring and autumn are the most popular times for visiting Kyoto and Nara. Reservations are essential. Winter is the ideal time to avoid the crowds. Summer is hot and sticky, but prime festival time. Summer is also when many Japanese visit Kōya-san, but numbers tail off in winter.

From Kansai International Airport (KIX) pass holders can take the **JR** to Ōsaka's JR Namba Station (one hour). To **Kyoto** the JR Haruka Limited Express takes 75 minutes. **Limousine bus** services from KIX to Ōsaka, Kyoto, Kōbe and Nara are slower than the train. All *Hikari* and *Kodama* **Shinkansen** services stop at Kyoto, Ōsaka, Kōbe and Himeji. For **Ise** take the Kintetsu line from Nagoya, Kyoto or Ōsaka. For Ama-no-hashidate there are direct JR trains from Kyoto and Ōsaka (the final section costs extra for JR pass holders).

Kyoto: Hankyū, Keihan and JR all have services between Ōsaka and Kyoto. Kintetsu provides a faster service than JR from Kyoto to **Nara**. Within Kyoto, the Keifuku line goes to **Arashiyama** and northwest Kyoto. The Eizan line from Demachi-yanagi goes to **Hiei-zan**. **Mampuku-ji** (Ōbaku Station) and **Byōdō-in** (Uji Station) are both on the JR Nara line. Kyoto has two subway lines. **Buses** are user-friendly and operate on a flat-fare system in town. A Kyoto Sightseeing or *Traffica* card can be used on both subways and buses. **Nara:** bus is the best option to Hōryū-ji from either the JR or Kintetsu stations. **Ōsaka:** for **Kōya-san** take the private Nankai Kōya line from Namba to Gokurakubashi then transfer to funicular.

Kyoto
LUXURY
The Screen, 640-1 Shimogoryomae-cho, Teramachi Marutamachi-sagaru, Nakagyo-ku, Kyoto, tel: 075 252 1113, www.the-screen.jp Luxury boutique hotel near to the Kyoto Imperial Palace.

MID-RANGE
Matsubaya Ryokan, Kyoto, tel: 075 351 3727, www.matsu bayainn.com Wooden ryokan, opened in 1885.
Ikoi No Ie Ryokan, 885 Ushitora-cho, Shimogyo-ku, tel: 075 354 8081, www.ikoi-no-ie.com Excellent location. Unusually for a *ryokan*, there is no curfew.

BUDGET
Guest Inn Kyoto, 174-5 Hanayacho Kushige Nishiiru Yakuencho Shimogyoku, tel: 075 341 1344, www.guest-inn-kyoto.jp Japanese-style rooms, low price and good location.

Nara
LUXURY
Nara Hotel, 1096 Takahata-chō, tel: 0742 26 3300, www.narahotel.co.jp/english/index.html Meiji Period elegance.

MID-RANGE
Kasuga Hotel, tel: 0742 22 4031, www.kasuga-hotel.co.jp Contemporary rooms, good open-air *onsen*, near to Kōfuki-ji Temple and Nara Park.

BUDGET
Yougendo, 13-25 Kudo 2-chome Oji-chō Kitakatsuragi-gun, Nara, tel: 074 532 0514, www.yougendo.com Great alternative to often crowded Nara accommodation.

Ōsaka
MID-RANGE
Carpe Diem, Nakahama 3 chome, 2-14 Joto-Ku (Midori-bashi station), tel: 06 6961 0444, www.carpediem-osaka.jp/en Lovely combination of city-centre location and traditional accommodation. Traditional arts courses offered.

Kōya-san
MID-RANGE
Over 50 temples offer *shukubō*-style lodgings at similar prices. Washing facilities are communal. *Shōjin-ryōri* (vegetarian cuisine) included. *See* Useful Contacts. **Rengejō-in**, tel: 0736 56 22 33, fax: 56 4743. Temple and lodgings founded in 1190.

Kyoto and Kinki at a Glance

WHERE TO EAT

Kyoto

Plenty of restaurants around Shijō-dōri and Kawaramachi-dōri. Narrow alleys of Pontocho are excellent for stumbling across good places to eat.

Gontara, Fuyacho-dori, Shijo-agaru, tel: 075 221 5801. Traditional noodle shop that has been serving loyal locals for over 80 years. Very good value.

Kitcho, Arashiyama Kitcho, 58 Susukinobaba, Saga Tenryuji, tel: 075 361 4401, www.kitcho.com/kyoto/english If you're staying somewhere modest, splash out here, at one of Kyoto's best restaurants.

Safera Bar Satonaka, 17 Benzaiten-cho, Higashiyama-ku, tel: 81 75 532 1139, www.ricordi-sfera.com Michito Satonaka runs this sleek bar in the Sfera building. Excellent drinks menu and good food.

Nara

The streets around Sanjō-dōri have a variety of restaurants. **Hirasō**, 30-1 Imanikado-chō (south of Sarusawa-ike). *Kaki-no-ha* (persimmon-wrapped) sushi and other specialities.

Ōsaka

Shinsaibashi, Namba and Umeda all teem with restaurants and cafés. Specialities include *Tako-yaki* (octopus balls) and *okonomiyaki*.

SHOPPING

Fureaikan (**Kyoto Museum of Traditional Crafts**), Basement of Miyako Messe Building, Nijō-dōri (just south of Heian Jingū). Purely viewing. Free admission, open 09:00–17:00, Tue–Sun.

Kyoto Handicraft Centre, Heian Jingū Kita, Marutamachi-dōri. Open 10:00–18:00, daily. The centre offers a wide range of traditional crafts for sale, as well as demonstration classes.

Yamato Mingei-ten, next to Maruzen (*see* below). Pottery, textiles, and paper from all over Japan.

Maruzen Book Store, located on Kawaramachi-dōri, north of Takoyakushi. Books and Japan Craft Centre are on the 4th floor. Open 10:00–20:00. Closed 3rd Wed of the month.

TOURS AND EXCURSIONS

JTB Kansai Sunrise Centre, tel: 075 341 1413, for Sunrise Tours with English-speaking guide in Kyoto, Nara, Ōsaka and excursions to Mount Yoshino and Ise.

Kyoto Specialist Guide Group, tel: 0773 64 0033, for specialist tours and guides.

JNTO Tourist Information Centre, Kansai International Airport, tel: 0724 56 6025. Open 09:00–21:00, daily.

USEFUL CONTACTS

Kyoto

For information visit http://kyotoguide.com and **Kyoto City Tourist Information**, 2F, JR Kyoto Station, tel: 075 343 6655. Open 08:30–19:00. **Kyoto Tourist Information Centre**, 9F, JR Kyoto Station, tel: 075 344 3300. Open 10:00–18:00.

Nara

City Tourist Information Centre, Sanjō-dōri (en route to Kōfuku-ji), tel: 0742 22 5595 (English-speaking service). Open 09:00–21:00, daily. Arrange guided walks.

Ōsaka

Ōsaka Human Rights Museum (Liberty Ōsaka),3-6-36 Naniwa-nishi, Naniwa-ku, Ōsaka 556 0026, tel: 06 6561 5891. Nearest station: Ashiharabashi, JR Kanko line.

Ōsaka Aquarium: www.kaiyukan.com

Kōya-san Tourist Association, 600 Kōya-san, Kōya-chō, Ito-gun Wakayama Prefecture, tel: 0736 56 2616, fax: 56 2889. Will help with *shukubō* reservations, www.shukubo.jp/eng/index.html

KYOTO	J	F	M	A	M	J	J	A	S	O	N	D
AVERAGE TEMP. °C	4	5	8	14	19	22	27	28	23	17	12	7
AVERAGE TEMP. °F	39	41	46	57	66	72	81	82	73	63	54	45
RAINFALL mm	50	66	111	152	154	248	235	143	203	112	70	40
RAINFALL in	2.0	2.6	4.4	6.0	6.1	9.8	9.3	5.6	8.0	4.4	2.8	1.6
DAYS OF RAINFALL	5	7	12	8	5	14	7	10	12	8	8	2

6
Western Honshū and Shikoku

The **San-in Coast**, as the Sea of Japan coast is known, means the north, or shadow side of the mountains. City dwellers wax lyrical about the area's natural beauty. Like the aristocrats of Heian Japan, however, they would not dream of living there; the sand dunes of Tottori are exotic, but bleak – the melancholy stuff of novels and films, not of real life.

Like Tōhoku, Western Honshū has managed to preserve the atmosphere of its castle towns without too much packaging. **Matsue**, Lafcadio Hearn's spiritual home, and **Hagi**, which spawned architects of the Meiji Revolution like Yoshida Shōin, are well worth visiting; so are **Tsuwano**, to the southeast of Matsue, and **Bitchū Takahashi**, north of Okayama.

Allied forces in World War II reserved their wrath for cities on the more heavily urbanized San-yō Coast facing the Inland Sea. No journey through Japan should exclude a visit to either the **Hiroshima Peace Memorial Museum** or the **Nagasaki Atomic Bomb Museum**. Both give a grim, but balanced, account of atomic devastation in the context of the Pacific War.

Shikoku is small, but stands up for itself. Kagawa, Tokushima, Kōchi and Ehime prefectures stamp their own cultures with their old names of Sanuki, Awa, Tosa and Iyo respectively. Moreover, Shikoku is the metaphorical birthplace of the hot spring (*onsen*) and of Kūkai, founder of Shingon Buddhism. **Matsuyama** and **Takamatsu** have the most to offer in the north, but the south coast is particularly attractive, and Tosa seafood is divine.

DON'T MISS

★★★ Hiroshima Peace Memorial Park: a sober reminder of nuclear horror.
★★★ Miyajima: one of Japan's three top scenic spots.
★★★ Lafcadio Hearn Memorial Museum: a pilgrimage to melancholy Matsue.
★★★ Bitchū Takahashi: tiny Zen garden of Raikyū-ji.
★★★ Dōgo Onsen Honkan: ultimate Japanese bathhouse.
★★★ Ritsurin Park: a large Edo Period garden.
★★ Izumo Taisha: Japan's second most sacred shrine.
★★ Hagi: old castle town.

Opposite: *Hiroshima Peace Memorial Park – cenotaph to victims of the 1945 bomb.*

Below: *Sumō wrestlers in ceremonial costume.*

SAN-IN COAST

The town of **Matsue** is one of the highlights of the San-in coast. Other places worth visiting include **Izumo** and the 17th-century **Hinomisaki Shrine** at Cape Hino, which also boasts Asia's oldest lighthouse. Political rebellion and pottery are **Hagi's** greatest claims to fame.

Matsue ★★★

Matsue is not Venice, although a boat ride along the Horikawa Moat encircling the squat, menacing presence of **Matsue Castle** is pleasant enough. Open 08:30–18:30 in summer (17:30 in winter), admission ¥550. *Kyōdō-ryōri*, the local cuisine based on seven types of seafood, is delicious. **Lake Shinji**, which is not far away, is a real draw, with plenty of boat tours and the lovely Vogel Park aviary.The real drawcard, however, is Lafcadio Hearn, an enigmatic, rather irascible, late 19th-century romantic who had the kind of love-hate relationship with Japan that many foreign residents experience.

Hearn lived in Matsue in 1890–91 before the cold winters drove him south to Kumamoto. Matsue, however, remained his spiritual home. The **Lafcadio Hearn Memorial Museum** (Koizumi Yakumo Kinen-kan) is lovingly curated by Hearn's great-grandson; items displayed include Hearn's old desk, numerous family pictures and some immaculate first editions. The display is well labelled in English. Open 08:30–17:00, daily (open until 18:30 April–September).

Next door, in the quiet beauty of Hearn's **Old Residence** it is not too difficult to imagine the owner, blind in one eye, squinting out into the garden for literary inspiration. It is open daily, 09:00–17:00. For a grander glimpse of the past, take a stroll past the **Buke Yashiki** (Samurai Residence) nearby. The **Adachi Museum of Art**,

in the town of Yasugi, is very close to Matsue and is worth visiting (see panel on page 102).

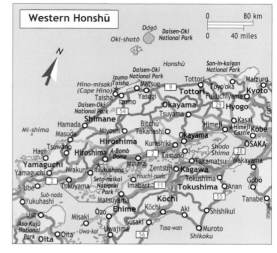

Izumo Taisha ★★

Izumo Taisha (Grand Shrine) is Japan's second most sacred shrine. At 24m (79ft), the **Honden** (Main Hall) of 1744 is a fraction of its original height; even so it is the tallest in Japan. Although the inner sanctum remains off limits, Izumo is more accessible and more satisfying than Ise. As the home of Ōkuninushi (the kami of fortune and marriage), Izumo Taisha is a particularly popular wedding venue, especially during October and November, when all eight million kami arrive at the **Kamiari-sai**, one of Japan's biggest Shinto rites.

Hagi ★★

This small, seaside Jōka-machi (castle town) west of Matsue was ruled by the Mōri family during the Edo Period. It is best explored at leisure by bicycle. The moss-covered tombs of the lords of Mōri at Tōkō-ji, an Ōbaku Zen temple, are especially atmospheric.

Several attractive samurai residences remain in the Jōka-machi area. There are also memorials to leaders of the Meiji Restoration like the fiery Yoshida Shōin (1830–59) and Itō Hirobumi (1841–1909), Japan's first prime minister. Both the Shōin Shrine and Ito's thatched-roofed house are well worth seeing. Hagi Castle was dismantled in 1874 as a symbol of allegiance to the new Meiji government; only the walls remain.

Further inland, the small samurai town of **Tsuwano** is famed for its Sagi-mai (White Heron Dance) which is performed every year on 20 and 27 July. This Shinto rite

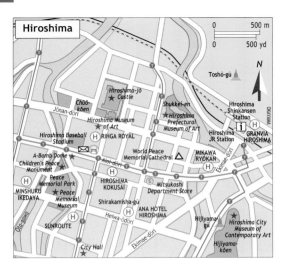

Hiroshima

0 — 500 m
0 — 500 yd

N

Toshō-gū

Hiroshima-jō Castle ★
Chūo-kōen
Jōnan-dōri
Hiroshima Museum of Art ★
Hiroshima Baseball Stadium ★
RIHGA ROYAL (H)
Shukkei-en
★Hiroshima Prefectural Museum of Art
Hiroshima Shinkansen Station
Hiroshima JR Station
GRANVIA HIROSHIMA
OKAYAMA
A-Bomb Dome ★
Children's Peace Monument
Aioi-dōri
World Peace Memorial Cathedral △
MIKAWA RYOKAN
Peace Memorial Park (H)
HIROSHIMA KOKUSAI
Mitsukoshi Department Store
Ekimae-dōri
MINSHUKU IKEDAYA
★ Peace Memorial Museum
Shirakamisha-sha
(H)
SUNROUTE
Heiwa-ōdōri
ANA HOTEL HIROSHIMA
Ōtagawa
Hijiyama-gū
Hiroshima City Museum of Contemporary Art ★
City Hall ★
Ekimae-dōri
Hijiyama-kōen

---

was imported from Kyoto in the 16th century and reintroduced to Kyoto in the 1950s. It is also famous for its 65,000 colourful *koi*, which outnumber the local population ten to one!

SAN-YŌ COAST

Okayama is a good base for visiting Kurashiki and for travelling across the country to Matsue. En route to Matsue lies a charming hotchpotch of temples and a small samurai quarter, **Bitchū-Takahashi**. Just west of Okayama lies **Kurashiki**.

The **Okayama Museum** houses an excellent art collection, including some Islamic art. *See* www.city.okayama.jp/orientmuseum

Kōraku-en ★★

Okayama's own highlight is **Kōraku-en,** considered one of Japan's top three gardens. Established by Ikeda Tsunamasa in 1686, Kōraku-en has an unusual mix of lawns, tea houses and even incudes a small tea plantation. However, it somehow lacks the charm of Kenroku-en in Kanazawa. Open 09:00–17:00, daily.

Bitchū-Takahashi ★★★

In the early 17th century, Kobori Enshū (1579–1647) the great tea master and garden designer, took up residence in this small town near Okayama at the Zen temple of **Raikyū-ji**. The tiny, exquisite garden visible today, said to be his work, is an inspiring mix of rocks, sculpted azalea hedges and concentric circles of sand with Mount Atago as a backdrop. Above town, it is well worth hiking up to **Bitchū-Matsuyama Castle**, Japan's highest fortification at 478m (1568ft) on top of Mount Gagyū.

ADACHI MUSEUM

The Adachi Museum of Art, with its exquisitely landscaped gardens, bears testimony to the statement of **Adachi Zenko**, the museum's late founder, that 'the garden, so to speak, is a picture scroll'. Glimpsed from the galleries, each outdoor scene is like a painting. The art collections are heavily contemporary, including paintings by Yokoyama Taikan (1868–1958) and a ceramics hall celebrating the artist potters Kawai Kanjirō and Kitaoji Rosanjin. The museum, an hour from Matsue Station by bus, is open daily, 09:00–17:30, April–September; 09:00–17:00, October–March. Admission ¥2200; 50% off for foreign visitors. *See* www.adachi-museum.or.jp/e

Kurashiki ★★

Kurashiki's small **Bikan** historical district, centred on a willow-lined canal full of little museums and old ware-houses, has become more and more manicured over the years, rather like a pretty Cotswold village. The **Ōhara Museum of Art**, with around 3000 original Western paint-ings, is well worth visiting. It contains works by Degas, Picasso, Cezanne and Renoir, and has a striking Neo-Classical façade. Open 09:00–16:30, Tuesday–Sunday.

HIROSHIMA

At 08:15 on 6 August 1945, the atomic bomb *Little Boy* detonated over Hiroshima, a once innocuous castle town turned 20th-century military nerve centre. Buildings and inhabitants within a radius of 2km (1.3 miles) of the hypo-centre were instantly incinerated.

Though the garden of **Shukkei-en** and the **Hiroshima Prefectural Museum of Art** are admirable diversions, a visit to Hiroshima can have only one main purpose.

Hiroshima Peace Memorial Park and Museum ★★★

The buckled **Atomic Bomb Dome** – the only building deliberately left standing from 1945 – is a grim reminder of the past. Across the park are a number of other memorials, notably the **Children's Peace Monument** swathed in rainbows of folded paper cranes dedicated to Sasaki Sadako, a two-year-old at the time of the bombing, who contracted leukaemia in 1955.

Through the archway of the **Cenotaph** to the A-Bomb victims, the Atomic Dome looms like a grotesque Taj Mahal. Here, on 6 August each year, doves are released in a peace ceremony.

The **Peace Memorial Museum** was expanded in 1995 to commemorate the

Below: *Autumn glory in Miyajima's Momiji-dani (Maple Valley).*

Above: *The imposing torii of Miyajima's Itsukushima Shrine by night.*

50th anniversary of the bombing. The most noticeable improvement is in the labelling, which no longer gives an impression of linguistic whitewash. Open 08:30–18:00, March–November; 08:30–17:00, December–February; 08:30–19:00, August. *See* www.pcf.city.hiroshima.jp/top_e.html for more detailed opening times information.

Miyajima ★★★

Opposite Hiroshima, the bright vermilion *Ō-torii* (Grand Gate) heralds a magical vision at high tide, when **Itsukushima Shrine** appears to float in the sea. Itsukushima Shrine, closely associated with Taira Kiyomori (defeated by Minamoto Yoritomo at Dan-no-ura in 1185), hosts festivals throughout the year, notably the **Kangensai** on 17 June, with music played from boats decorated with lanterns. On 31 December there is a fire festival. Miyajima has various parks and temples, as well as deer and some rather vicious monkeys. Hiking up the 530m (1739ft) Misen-san is not particularly strenuous.

SHIKOKU

The island of Shikoku is divided into four prefectures: Kagawa (Sanuki), Tokushima (Awa), Kōchi (Tosa) and Ehime (Iyo). **Takamatsu City** in Kagawa Prefecture is the gateway to Shikoku from Okayama. **Naruto** in Tokushima Prefecture is the gateway to Shikoku from Kōbe: much is made of its whirlpools, where the Inland Sea and Pacific clash in the Naruto Straits, but these are not particularly dramatic unless the tides are right.

Ritsurin-kōen ★★★

Takamatsu City's principal claim to horticultural fame is **Ritsurin-kōen**, a beautiful Edo Period legacy boasting

---

INLAND SEA

For better or worse, a mind-boggling network of bridges now linking Shikoku with Honshū has made the Inland Sea islands of Ikuchijima and Ōmishima in the Geiyo Straits more accessible than ever before. Ikuchijima is famous for Kōsan-ji, a temple and museum complex with full-scale reproductions of temples and shrines from all over Japan. Ōmishima is renowned for its ancient Ōyamazumi Shrine and vast museum of armoury dating back to the 12th century – of interest mainly to military buffs.

six ponds, thirteen hills and fifteen bridges. Also worth visiting is the **Sanuki Folkcraft Museum**. The garden is open 06:00–18:00 and the museum is open 08:45–18:00, daily, year round.

Some of Kagawa Prefecture's other drawcards include Shikoku Mura at Yashima (east of Takamatsu City), with its outstanding collection of traditional architecture and a vine suspension bridge replicating the one across the Ōboke Gorge in Tokushima Prefecture. **Zentsū-ji**, temple number 75 on the 88-Temple Pilgrimage, is the birthplace of Kūkai.

Kotohira-gū ★★

This ancient shrine in Kagawa Prefecture, second in popularity only to Ise and Izumo, has a chequered religious history as both a temple and a shrine dedicated to the kami of seafarers and fishermen. Its popular name of **Kompira-san** derives from **Kumbhira**, the crocodile god of the Ganges, who was absorbed into both the Buddhist and Shinto pantheon.

Do not let yourself be put off by the 30-minute climb up the steps to the main buildings, where the **Ema-dō** (Votive Plaque Hall) houses an extraordinary mishmash of plaques and model ships left here to ensure safety on the seas.

Tokushima City ★★

Tokushima City is famous for its **Bunraku** puppet theatre. In August the streets throb to the beat of drums and bells as teams of Awa dancers strut their stuff during the **Bon Festival**. **Awa Odori** is a hypnotically inane shuffle said to have been started during a drunken party to celebrate the completion of Tokushima Castle in

88-TEMPLE PILGRIMAGE

Shikoku is the smallest of Japan's four main islands, but has the longest pilgrimage of all: a 1200km (750-mile) circuit of 88 temples throughout all four prefectures. The pilgrimage was initiated in honour of Kūkai, the founder of Shingon Buddhism, who was born at Zentsū-ji near Takamatsu and found enlightenment at Cape Murato. The circuit starts at Ryōzen-ji in Naruto City and progresses clockwise, ending at Ōkubo-ji in Nagao, Kagawa Prefecture. Pilgrims dress in white and carry a staff. For many, the journey is another form of group travel.

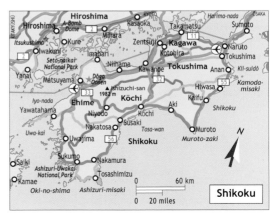

Above: *A mouthwatering array of fresh sushi including maki (rolls) and nigiri (bite-sized pieces of fish on rice).*
Opposite: *Dōgo Onsen once played host to emperors. Today, it is a venerable public bathhouse.*

1585. There seems little reason to dispute this story.

Tokushima Prefecture is also Shikoku's **crafts** capital, famous in particular for indigo, handmade paper and Ōtani pottery.

Kōchi City ★★

Kōchi City is street-market mad, every day of the week. The biggest is the Sunday market on Ōte-suji by the main gate of Kōchi Castle, brimming with stalls selling a hotchpotch of fresh produce and bric-a-brac. Kōchi also has a good **Museum of Art** (modern) and a **Botanical Garden** well befitting its near-tropical climate.

Tosa food should be high on anyone's menu in Japan. **Sawachi cuisine** consists of huge platters bulging with *sashimi*, *tataki* (seared bonito) and *sushi*. In August, Kōchi City stages the **Yosakoi Matsuri**, a lively, carnival-type festival meaning 'Come on Over Tonight!' The festival was apparently devised as a way of lifting people's spirits during the 1950s. Thousands of dancers team up, turning out in a variety of costumes; there are also a number of rock, reggae and samba bands.

Kōchi City sits at the centre of Tosa Bay, which arches east to Cape Muroto and west to **Cape Ashizuri**. With all due respect to the monk Kūkai, who found enlightenment at Muroto, the lighthouse on the blustery cliffs at Ashizuri, the most southerly point on Shikoku, is a more dramatic option. Here, Kongōfuku-ji, devoted to Kannon, is the 38th temple on the 88-Temple Pilgrimage (*see* panel, page 105).

Matsuyama Castle ★★★

The capital of Ehime is Matsuyama. **Matsuyama Castle**, above the town, is among the most beautiful in Japan, despite various bouts of reconstruction since the early 17th century. In clear weather there are great views from the top of the *donjon* across to Ishizuchi-san and the Inland Sea. Other nearby attractions include the

Shinonome Shrine, which hosts torch-lit Nō performances in April, and the **Bansui-sō**, an exotic villa at the bottom of the hill built in the 1920s.

Dōgo Onsen ★★★

Dōgo, near Matsuyama, is the 'oldest' hot spring in Japan, first mentioned in 8th-century chronicles. Since then it has played host to emperors, feudal lords and commoners alike. The **Dōgo Onsen Honkan** is virtually the grandfather of the **public bathhouse** (sentō) still found all over Japan. It has three classes of service: no-frills bathing only on the first floor; bathing on the first floor, plus relaxation with tea in a yukata (see panel) on the second floor, or a private room with tea on the third floor. To take a peek at the Imperial Baths costs extra.

Today's magnificent building dates from 1894. Its decorative heron motif recalls the bird that 'discovered' the spring by healing its injured leg in the waters. Dōgo is noisy and crowded but, like a good Turkish Bath, not to be missed. Open 06:30–23:00.

Ishite-ji (Stone Hand Temple) ★★

Ishite, the 51st temple on the 88-Temple Pilgrimage near Dōgo, is Shikoku's weirdest. As well as having some fine Kamakura Period architecture, it also has a disco-land of flashing Buddhist images in tunnels guaranteed to make Shikoku's venerable son, Kūkai, turn in his grave on Kōya-san.

Ishizuchi-san ★★

At 1982m (6503ft), Ishizuchi-san is Shikoku's highest and most sacred mountain, where **yamabushi** and **pilgrims** flock in early July. A ropeway up to 1300m (4265ft) cuts out a lot of the hard work, but the proper pilgrim's route involves climbing up the rock face on chains; this can be as slow a process as climbing Mount Fuji, but it is not particularly arduous. There is also an easier route not involving chains.

Western Honshū and Shikoku at a Glance

The weather on the San-in Coast is unpredictable at any time of year. August is busy in Hiroshima, due to the annual memorial service on the 6th, and also in Tokushima during the Bon Festival. Make reservations well in advance. Spring and autumn are the best times to avoid the heat.

Hagi on the **San-in Coast** is best reached by JR from Shimonoseki. JR from Okayama is also the quickest way to **Matsue** via both Kurashiki and **Bitchū Takahashi**. The other option is to fly to Izumo or Yonago. **The San-yō Coast** is well serviced by Shinkansen. **Tsuwano** is best reached via JR from Ogōri on the Shinkansen line. The fastest route to **Matsuyama** is by hydrofoil from Hiroshima, or take the Nishi Seto Expressway from Onomichi to Imabari. There are road and rail links from Okayama to **Takamatsu** (Seto-Ōhashi line) and from Kōbe, via Awaji-shima, to Naruto. There are also **air services** to Shikoku's main cities and ferry services from Kyūshū.

San-in Coast: in Matsue it is worth hiring a **bicycle** at the station and buying a **Universal Pass** to the main sights. The most convenient route to **Izumo Taisha** is the Ichibata line from Matsue Onsen

Station. Since Hagi is spread out it is best seen by bicycle. **San-yō Coast**: The **Bikan** district of **Kurashiki** is a short walk from Kurashiki Station (not Shin-Kurashiki Station, which is the Shinkansen stop). **Hiroshima** has a user-friendly **tram** system which operates on a flat-fare system in the centre. Trams No. 2 and No. 6 are on the **Peace Park** route. A JR pass is valid on ferries from Hiroshima to Miyajima. Ōmishima and Ikuchijima in the **Inland Sea** can also be reached by ferry from Ono-michi in Hiroshima Prefecture or on a hydrofoil tour from Miyajima.

Shikoku: there are reasonable bus and rail services across the island, however, a car is use-ful, particularly for exploring the coast. For **Dōgo Onsen** take the tram from Matsuyama.

Matsue
LUXURY
Minami-kan, 14 Suetsugu Honmachi, Matsue City, Shimane Prefecture, tel: 0852 21 5131, fax: 26 0351. Classy *ryokan*, with good location. Convenient for Matsue Castle area. Excellent *Kyōdō-ryōri*.

BUDGET
Ryokan Terazue, 60-3 Tenjin-machi, Matsue, tel: 0852 21 3480. Modest but very friendly *ryokan*. Could do with a fresh lick of paint in places, but well located and good value.

Hagi
LUXURY
Hokumon Yashiki, 210 Hori-uchi, Hagi City, tel: 0838 22 75 21. Charming *ryokan*, appropriate for a castle town.

Kurashiki
MID-RANGE
Hagihonjin Spa, 385-8 Chinto, Hagi-shi Yamaguchi-ken, tel: 0838 758 1157, www.hagihonjin.co.jp/spa A lovely place to stay, tradi-tional Japanese feel, with excellent *onsen* facilities.

Okayama Prefecture
MID-RANGE
Okayama International Villa Group, Okayama International Centre, 2-2-1 Hokanchō, Okayama 700, tel: 086 256 2535, www.harenet. ne.jp/villa Six villas for rent.

Hiroshima
LUXURY
Granvia Hiroshima, 1-5 Matsubara-cho, Minami-Ku, Hiroshima 732-0822, tel: 082 262 1111, www.hgh.co.jp/ english/index.html One of the nicest hotels in this small, upmarket chain. Close to the Memorial Peace Park.

BUDGET
World Friendship Centre (**WFC**), 8-10 Higashi-Kannon-machi, Nishi-ku, Hiroshima City, 733-0032, tel: 082 503 3191, www.wfchiroshima.net Japanese-style rooms. American-inspired, aimed at

Western Honshū and Shikoku at a Glance

cultural understanding. Convenient for Peace Park.
Minshuku Ikedaya, 6-36 Dobashi-chō, Naka-ku, Hiroshima City 730, tel: 082 231 3329, fax: 231 7875. Near Peace Park, friendly.

Miyajima
MID-RANGE
Hotel Makoto, 755 Miyajima-cho, Hatsukaichi-shi, tel: 0829 44 0070. *Ryokan*, five minutes' walk from the station; good *onsen*. Excellent fresh seafood.

Shikoku–Matsuyama
LUXURY
Funaya, 1-33 Yunochō, Dōgo, Matsuyama City, tel: 0899 47 0278. One of the finest *ryokan* in Dōgo.

Takamatsu
MID-RANGE
Hotel Bokaiso, Yashima Yamagami, Takamatsu-shi, tel: 087 841 9111. The views make staying here worthwhile – on a hill overlooking the city and the Seto Inland Sea. Good *onsen*.

Kōchi
Nansui Ryokan, 1-7-12 Kaminachi, Kochi-dhi, tel: 088 837 2181, www.nansui.ne.jp Good food, particularly the local speciality of *sawachi* (sushi, sashimi and tataki presented on a large, colourful platter).

For excellent *Kyōdō-ryōri* reserve at Minami-kan. In **Hagi** try the Teramachi area and

Tamachi Arcade. In **Okayama** there are several restaurants in Hotel Granvia and the streets east of the station. **Kurashiki** has coffee shops and restaurants in the Bikan district and, at night, around the station.

Hiroshima
Hondori offers many choices. For *okonomiyaki* try **Okonomimura**, 5-13 Shin-tenchi (off Chūō-dōri). Also **Viale** (Italian) and **Kisui** (*shabu-shabu*), **Hotel Sunroute**, 15th floor.
Bien Dinner Bar, 1F, 10-13 Mikawa-cho, Naka-ku, Hiroshima-shi. Well located on Peace Avenue. Very friendly, with laid-back atmosphere.

Shikoku-Takamatsu
Zaigoudon Waraya, 91 Yachima-Nakamachi, tel: 087 843 3115. 100-year-old thatched-roof noodle restaurant; near entrance to Shikoku Mura.

Kōchi City
Kuroshio Ichiba, 1-6-1 Harimaya-cho, Harimayabashi Shotengai, tel: 088 885 9640. Stylish izakaya known for its local delicacy, *katsuo no tataki* (half-smoked bonito fish).

Matsuyama
Ōkaidō, south of the castle, has a large choice of eateries.

Matsue: Horikawa Moat Tour. Departs Matsukawa Horikawa Fureai Square and Karakoro Square every 15 minutes, 09:00–17:00.
JTB Kansai Sunrise Centre, tel: 075 341 1413. Tours of Hiroshima, Kurashiki, Miyajima from Kyoto and Ōsaka.
World Friendship Centre (*see* Where to Stay) arranges meetings with A-bomb survivors, as well as guided tours.

Matsue
Tourist Information Centre (Matsue Stn), tel: 0852 21 4034.
Hagi
Tourist Information at both Higashi Hagi and Hagi stations.
Hiroshima
Hiroshima City Tourist Association, by Motoyasu Bridge in Peace Park, tel: 082 247 6738. **Tourist Information Centre** (Takamatsu Stn), tel: 087 851 2009. Open 09:30–18:00 (April–September); 09:30–19:00 (15 August); 8:30–17:00 (October–March).
Matsuyama
Ehime Prefectural International Centre, 1-1 Dōgo Ichiman, tel: 089 917 5678. *See also* www.epic.or.jp/english/index.html

HIROSHIMA	J	F	M	A	M	J	J	A	S	O	N	D
AVERAGE TEMP. °C	6	6	9	14	19	23	27	28	24	18	13	8
AVERAGE TEMP. °F	43	43	48	57	66	73	81	82	75	64	55	46
RAINFALL mm	60	74	127	140	156	232	258	142	173	76	64	33
RAINFALL in	2.4	2.9	5.0	5.5	6.1	9.1	10.2	5.6	6.8	3.0	2.5	1.3
DAYS OF RAINFALL	3	8	10	9	7	14	11	12	14	5	6	3

7
Kyūshū and Okinawa

The rocky, island-studded coast of Kyūshū has greeted visitors since at least the 3rd century BC. **Koreans**, **Portuguese**, **Dutch** and **Chinese** all arrived here first; so did Buddhism, Christianity, guns, medicine, and porcelain. No port acted more hospitably than **Nagasaki**, which makes it doubly cruel that when America came calling in 1945, it was to drop an atomic bomb. Nagasaki retains a fascinating mix of Chinese and European influences reflected even in its festivals.

Sakurajima, smoking out in Kagoshima Bay, is a striking reminder of Kyūshū's vulnerability to natural explosive forces. At **Beppu**, bubbling mud, hot sand and palm trees are harnessed to create the ultimate Japanese spa town; **Ibusuki** is somewhat less tacky. Much wilder altogether is **Kirishima-Yaku National Park**.

The **Ryūkyū Islands** (Okinawa Prefecture) are truly subtropical with coral reefs and white beaches, yet this once independent kingdom has long been a pawn: from the 14th century it paid tribute to the Chinese; in 1609 it was annexed by Satsuma in southern Kyūshū; in World War II it found itself cornered in a bloody battle zone. From 1945–72 it belonged to the USA. Today, firmly back on Japan's side of the board, American military bases remain.

The Okinawans are ethnically closer to the Japanese than the Ainu. Their culture has also fared better: local arts, textiles, crafts and festivals still thrive. The biggest attraction is the wealth of **beaches** and **diving** opportunities on the **outer islands**, not to mention the exotic flora and fauna of **Iriomote**.

DON'T MISS

★★★ **Canal City Fukuoka:** 21st-century Japan at its best.
★★★ **Nagasaki Atomic Bomb Museum:** a dramatic, disturbing reminder of 1945.
★★★ **Kirishima-Yaku National Park:** volcanoes and natural beauty without Mount Aso's heavy tourism.
★★★ **Yaeyama Islands:** wildlife on Iriomote and diving off Yonaguni.
★★ **Hirado:** historic island associated with Christianity.
★★ **Ibusuki:** bath in sand.
★★ **Sakurajima:** volcanic encounter off Kagoshima.

Opposite: *Taketomi Island, haven of Okinawan architecture.*

Below: *Soviet-donated
'Peace' sculpture in
Nagasaki Peace Park.*

FUKUOKA AND ENVIRONS

Over the past few years, **Fukuoka** has turned from a dingy
city into a highly sophisticated metropolis spilling out into
the bay, where the 234m (768ft) **Fukuoka Tower** soars sky-
wards. South of the city, the historic towns of **Dazaifu** and
Yanagawa are well worth a visit.

Fukuoka Canal City ★★★

The truly chic part of Fukuoka is Canal City, close to Hakata
Station. This curvaceous, dusky pink and magenta hotel,
shopping and theatre complex demonstrates the latest **urban
architecture**. (It cost US$1.4 billion to build and was privately
funded). At night the lanterns of *yatai* (food stalls) beckon
cheerfully along the Naka-gawa. *See* www.canalcity.co.jp/eg

The Momochi district around the waterfront is very
pretty, with lots of parks, wide streets, and the Fukuoka
Dome baseball stadium. A great place for a stroll.

Dazaifu ★★

Dazaifu's main attraction is the flamboyant shrine of
Tenman-gū, dedicated to **Sugawara Michizane**, kami
of learning, who died here in AD903 (*see* page 13). The
present building dates from the Momoyama Period,
although tradition has it that the **Flying Plum** tree on the
right of the courtyard uprooted itself to join Michizane in
exile all those centuries ago. Also worth visiting in Dazaifu
are the Zen garden of **Kōmyōzen-ji** and **Kanzeon-ji**.

Yanagawa ★★

The Venice of Japan title goes to Yanagawa, an old castle
town with **willow-lined canals**. A boat (or, more strictly
speaking, a punt) trip here, combined with the historical
sights, makes a good day trip from Fukuoka.

NAGASAKI AND BEYOND

Had the skies over Kokura been clear on 9 August 1945,
Nagasaki might have escaped decimation; but it was
bombed by bad luck and only ever gets a mention as an
addendum to Hiroshima. As if to compensate, the city
abounds in memorials of Soviet proportions, notably

Kitamura Seibō's **Peace Statue**, one hand pointing skyward and the other holding back evil, and at Fukusai-ji, a gigantic Kannon-cum-Virgin Mary.

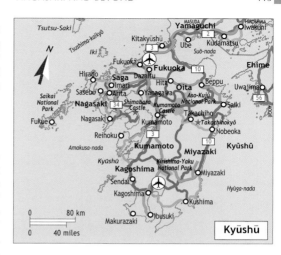

Nagasaki Atomic Bomb Museum ★★★

The A-bomb sites, which include the **Peace Park** and **Urakami Cathedral**, are in the northern area of Urakami, where the bomb detonated. The **Nagasaki Atomic Bomb Museum** is high on drama compared to Hiroshima: the display begins with a clock ticking until the deadly moment of 11:02, on 9 August 1945. As at Hiroshima, the linguistic whitewash has now disappeared: specific mentions are given to the minorities who died, including forced labourers and prisoners of war. Open 08:30–17:30, admission ¥200. *See* www1.city.nagasaki.nagasaki.jp/peace/index_e.html

Central Nagasaki ★★

Central Nagasaki is compact enough to see on foot. Just west of Nishi-zaka, beneath a Gaudi-esque church spire, is the **Twenty-six Martyrs' Memorial** to a group of mission-aries and Japanese converts crucified in 1597. The mood gets no jollier walking in the shadow of the gigantic Kannon through the graveyards of Fukusai-ji and Shōfuku-ji. At the eastern end, however, nowhere could be more lively than **Suwa Shrine** in October during the **Kunchi Festival**.

Chinatown is less atmospheric than in Yokohama, but worth a visit. So, too, are Kōfuku-ji and Sōfuku-ji in Teramachi, both Ōbaku Zen temples founded in the 1620s by the Chinese. Also picturesque is **Megane-bashi** (Spectacles Bridge), Japan's oldest stone bridge, built in 1634. The history of **Dejima**, an artificial island where the Dutch were confined

---

JAPANESE PORCELAIN

In 1615, the Korean potter, Ri Sanpei, discovered kaolin near Arita in northwest Kyūshū. By the 1650s, porcelain had become a major export indus-try. The main styles were **blue and white**, old *Imari* (blue, red and gold), *Kakiemon*, (delicate bird and flower designs) and *Nabeshima* (made purely for the local lords). The kiln village of Ōkawachi-yama (outside Imari) is a charming maze of shops. Items range from cheap, but attractive bowls to vastly expensive, modern *Nabeshima* wares. Arita abounds with kiln sites and collections. For the best overview go to the Kyūshū Ceramic Museum. Open 09:00–16:30, Tuesday–Sunday. Each year there is also an Arita Porcelain Fair from 29 April to 5 May.

Nagasaki

from the 1640s to the 1850s, has now been restored, and it has become part of the main town as the surrounding area was reclaimed during the 20th century. Museums, shops and recreations of the original Dutch houses are open for visitors. Open 08:00–18:00, admission ¥500.

South Nagasaki ★★

The main sights in the south part of Nagasaki are European-inspired, apart from the highly exotic **Con-fucian Shrine** (**Kōshi-byō**), tucked beneath Oranda-zaka (the Dutch slopes). The shrine's museum has fine displays of treasures from the Palace Museum in Beijing.

Glover Garden is named after Thomas Glover, a 19th-century entrepreneur who helped provide arms to supporters of the Meiji Restoration. He also married a *geisha*, who was widely believed to have been the inspiration behind Puccini's **Madama Butterfly**. It is well worth seeing the garden's fine Meiji Period houses, though the escalators up the hill spoil the landscaping. Open daily 08:00–21:30 in summer, until 18:00 in winter, admission ¥500. By the gardens is the small 19th-century Gothic-style **Ōura Catholic Church**.

Hirado ★★

The island of **Hirado** is the complete antithesis to **Huis Ten Bosch**, a high-tech replica of 17th-century Holland between Nagasaki and Sasebo crammed with windmills, amusements and top-class hotels. The settlement of Hirado itself has only the ruins of a 17th-century Dutch settlement, a reconstructed castle and a pleasant shopping street; its real highlight is a magical view of the St Francis Xavier Memorial Church

Opposite: *The Inari Shrine in Kumamoto is one of thousands across Japan associated with the fox.*

THE CHRISTIAN CENTURY (1549–1639)

Japan probably had 300,000 converts at the peak of its turbulent Christian century. In 1639, after an uprising by Christians and peasants of Shimabara, Tokugawa Iemitsu banned Christianity. In Kyūshū (and on Hirado) this resulted in enclaves of hidden Christians who took Japanese religious syncretism to new heights by worshipping the Buddhist goddess **Kannon** as the Virgin Mary and **Jizō**, Saviour of Children, as Jesus.

peeking across the roofs of Buddhist temples. The city of Hirado was enlarged in 2005 by merging with local towns. It is still a very pretty place, and very open and friendly to foreign visitors. The beaches are also worth a visit.

Other low-key attractions include **Sakikata Park**, the quiet resting place of **Will Adams** (Anjin Miura), an English sailor shipwrecked in 1600, best known to the world as the hero of James Clavell's bestseller *Shōgun*. The **Hirado Tourist Museum** (devoted largely to Christian relics) and the **Matsuura Museum** are worth visiting.

FROM BEPPU TO IBUSUKI

Beppu is Las Vegas kitsch minus the casinos. **Ibusuki** is less tacky and a good deal balmier, being halfway to Okinawa. In between lie Kyūshū's two national parks.

Beppu ★

Beppu boasts 2849 hot springs gushing 136,000kl (36 million gallons) of water a day plus nine *jigoku* (hells) of bubbling mud and geysers. The three best 'hells' are **Umi Jigoku**, a beautiful, boiling hot azure pool, **Bōzu Jigoku** (Monk's Hell), a stinking, belching mud pool resembling a priest's shaven head and **Chi-no-ike** (Pond of Blood), tinged rusty with iron oxide. If you cannot get to Ibusuki in the far south, take a sand bath at **Takegawara Onsen**.

A much more refined spa alternative is **Yufuin**, situated on a pretty plateau about an hour from Beppu. Another option is a visit to **Usuki**, home to 60 remarkable 12–14th-century Buddhas carved, mostly in groups, out of freestanding rock and into the surrounding hillsides. The Usuki Buddhas were designated National Treasures in 1995 after an extensive restoration programme.

Kumamoto ★

Kumamoto Castle is Japan's third biggest and one of its most romantic-looking by night. It was used during the filming of Tom Cruise's 2003 film, *The Last Samurai*. The other major attraction in town is **Suizenji-kōen**, an elaborate garden dating from 1632. This contains a

---

KYŪSHŪ CUISINE

The citizens of **Fukuoka** and **Beppu** love eating *fugu* (blowfish), which is toxic if its inner organs are not removed correctly. **Nagasaki** specialities include *shippoku-ryōri*, a Japanese version of Chinese cuisine with hints of Portuguese influence. **Kagoshima** specializes in *satsuma-ryōri*. Dishes include *satsuma-age* (deep-fried fish cake) and *kibinago sashimi* made from silvery sardines.

KYŪSHŪ FESTIVALS

• 3–4 May: **Hakata Dontaku** (Fukuoka). Colourful festival of folk origins.
• 1–15 July: **Hakata Gion Yamakasa** (Fukuoka). The climax on the 15th is a 5km (3-mile) race between teams carrying floats decked with giant dolls. Starts 04:59 at the Kushida Shrine.
• 28 July: **Onda Matsuri** at Aso Jinja. Features shrine maidens accompanying *mikoshi* and lion dances.
7–9 October: **Nagasaki Kunchi** at Suwa Shrine. Festival incorporates Dutch minstrels and lion dances. One of the liveliest in Kyūshū.
• Mid-November to mid-February: **Yo-kagura Festival** (Takachiho). Troupes of residents perform the 33 dances of the gods through the night.

series of scenes (including a miniature Mount Fuji) representing the 53 Stations of the Tōkaidō. The **Prefectural Traditional Crafts Centre** by the northeast gate of the Castle has a range of Kumamoto crafts.

Aso Kujū National Park ★★

The Yamanami highway from Beppu to Kumamoto is a scenic dream and a holiday-season nightmare. The highlight en route is the **Aso Caldera**, one of the world's largest volcanic craters, stretching 18km (11 miles) from west to east and 24km (15 miles) from north to south. Above the grassy highlands rise the five volcanic peaks that form Aso-san. The most active peak in recent years has been Naka-dake. The scale of the landscape is utterly compelling, but peering into Naka-dake's crater can be a vision of hell, both for the geological gurglings and the crowds.

Takachiho ★★

This small town in Miyazaki Prefecture is known for its beautiful gorge and mythological associations depicted in ancient ***kagura* dances** performed nightly (*see page 26*) from 20:00–21:00. According to the chronicles, the **grandson of Amaterasu** descended to earth in Kyūshū on a mountain

called Takachiho. The villagers do not seem to care that the most likely candidate for this hallowed spot is Takachiho-no-mine, a mountain in the Kirishima-Yaku National Park. Nevertheless, they can lay claim to the cave where Amaterasu took refuge.

Also in Miyazaki Prefecture, the **Nichinan Coast** makes a good diversion for its exotic 'washboard' rock formations between Cape Toi and Aoshima. This is the southernmost tip of the coast, and has spectacular scenery, with wild horses grazing (that are designated a natural monument) and an attractive lighthouse.

Sakurajima ★★

Kagoshima is worth a visit to ogle at Sakurajima, smoking out in Kagoshima Bay.

Sakurajima means 'Cherry Blossom Island', but rains more than pink petals: during eruptions it coats Kagoshima with dust. The one advantage is that Sakurajima's soil is so fertile that it can grow huge *daikon* (radishes). The **Sakurajima Visitor Centre** provides interesting information on the great 1914 eruption and also the latest seismic information. Open 09:00–17:00 Tue–Sun.

Kirishima-Yaku National Park ★★★

This wonderful national park has 23 volcanoes, 10 crater lakes, hiking trails galore, *onsen* and wildlife. Better still, it is not as tourist-ridden as Aso. The village of **Ebino Kōgen**, on a volcanic plateau, is the most convenient base for walking. From Karakuni-dake (a two-hour climb from Ebino Kōgen), there are great views towards Sakurajima. A much longer route will take you to the top of **Takachiho-no-mine**. Trails are generally well signposted, but ensure you have adequate water. Camping makes sense if you really want to get away from it all.

Ibusuki ★★

This beach is *the* place to have a sand bath. A mild attack of the giggles at the idea of being buried in a *yukata* by dour grannies is forgivable. But the oddly clogging sensation is relieved by the illusion afterwards of feeling as if you might have lost weight. The bathhouse by the beach is the best place to start this strange odyssey.

Chiran, between Ibusuki and Kagoshima, has a charming old samurai quarter from the days of the Shimazu lords of Satsuma. It is also where kamikaze pilots flew off on their organized death missions during 1944 and 1945. The **Chiran Peace Museum for Kamikaze Pilots** is a disturbing memorial to the single-mindedness of Japanese purpose directed the wrong way. In 2008, the museum added a touch-panel display system in both Japanese and English for a large selection of the kamikaze pilots' final letters, wills, poems etc. Open 09:00–17.00, admission ¥500.

Above: *Buried alive in a therapeutic sand bath.*
Opposite: *Festival dancing involves the whole community and can last for several days.*

YAKUSHIMA

Yakushima is around four hours south of Kagoshima by ferry and halfway to another planet. In the mountainous interior, where Mount Miyanoura rises to 1935m (6349ft), it rains, and rains to the tune of 10,000mm (394in) a year. In winter it snows high up. The island has different bands of vegetation, ranging from **subtropical** under 200m (656ft) to warm temperate between 200m (656ft) and 800m (2625ft). Above this band thrive the **Yaku-sugi**, cedar trees indigenous to Yakushima. One tree, called Jōmon-sugi, is estimated to be anywhere between 5000 and 7200 years old.

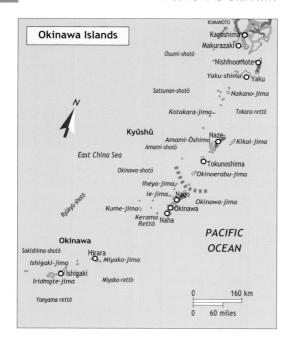

Okinawa Islands

KUMAMOTO
Kagoshima
Makurazaki
Osumi-shotō
Nishinoomote
Yaku-shima Yaku
Satsunan-shotō
Nakano-jima
Kotakara-jima
Tokara-rettō
Kyūshū
Naze
Amami-Ōshima Kikai-jima
Amami-shotō
East China Sea
Tokunoshima
Okinawa-shotō
Okinoerabu-jima
Iheya-jima
Ie-jima Nago
Ryūkyū-shotō
Okinawa-jima
Kume-jima Okinawa
Kerama Naha
Rettō
Okinawa
Sakishima-shotō
Hirara
Ishigaki-jima Miyako-jima
Ishigaki
Iriomote-jima Miyako-rettō
Yaeyama-rettō

PACIFIC
OCEAN

0   160 km
0   60 miles

Okinawa Island

South Okinawa was the scene of the bloodiest fighting of the Pacific War. **Himeyuri-no-tō** is a memorial to the 219 schoolgirls and teachers who committed suicide on 19 June 1945 to avoid capture. Today, looking out over the benign blue sea from **Mabuni-no-oka**, the scene of the final battle for Okinawa, it is hard to imagine the carnage that took place. South of Naha, the capital of Okinawa Prefecture, are the underground chambers that acted as the **Japanese Naval Headquarters**. Open 08:30–17:00.

In northern Okinawa, Nakagusuku is worth pausing at only to see the early 18th-century **Nakamura-ke** residence and 15th-century ruins of **Nakagusuku Castle**. Kadena Airbase is an eyesore. However, **Cape Hedo**, the northernmost point of Okinawa Island, is worth the drive. The northeast coast has pretty fishing villages such as Oku.

Naha ★

Naha is considered to be anomalous urban Japan, where each year on 10 October, the American bombing of the city in 1944 is commemorated by a tug-of-war contest.

Naha has plenty of bars and restaurants. The main **shopping** opportunities are on **Kokusai-dōri** (where you will find everything from crafts to boutiques) and along **Heiwa-dōri** and **Ichiba-dōri**, with its market area crammed full of fish and fruit.

The **Tsuboya** pottery area nearby has been around since 1682. The Tsuboya style influenced Hamada Shōji

---

RYŪKYŪ CUISINE AND TEXTILES

Although Ryūkyū cuisine uses a lot of fish, **pork** is popular too – everything from the ears to the trotters. *Champuru* is a thick stew of noodles and pork, or *goya* (bitter melon). Okinawa's most attractive crafts are its textiles. ***Bingata*** are stencil-dyed fabric in vibrant blues, red and yellows from Shuri, which ruled the Ryūkyū Kingdom from the 15–19th centuries. Kume-jima **silk** is expensive, but there is also a huge range of simple weaves.

in the 1920s (*see* page 46). The large, rustic storage jars are attractive but not very practical to transport.

Shuri-jō ★★★

Northeast of central Naha is Shuri-jō, a semi-Chinese structure that was the royal residence of the **Ryūkyū Dynasty**, founded in 1429. Though rebuilt in 1992, the flamboyant façade of vermilion and golden dragons is a faithful reproduction of the original style. Shuri-jō is the venue of Okinawa's **New Year** celebrations and the **Shuri-jō Festival** of 1–3 November. The **Okinawa Prefectural Museum** nearby is also worth a visit. The museum was relocated and re-opened in late 2007. The new address is 3-1-1 Omoromachi, Naha City; tel: 098 941 8200. Open: 09:00–18:00, Fri and Sat; 09:00–20:00, Tue–Sun. Admission is ¥400. *See* www.museums.pref.okinawa.jp/english/museum/index.html

Outer Islands ★★

The **Kerama Islands**, 35km (22 miles) off Okinawa Island, have unspoilt beaches and good diving. **Zamami-jima** is the home of Okinawa's **whale-watching** activities, which usually get into swing in late January. **Kume-jima** – out on a limb to the west – was the capital of the old Ryūkyū Kingdom's **silk production**: silk making can still be observed in Nakazato village. The low-lying Miyako Islands are 330km (205 miles) south of Okinawa Island. **Miyako-jima** is renowned for its beaches and nightlife.

Yaeyama Islands ★★★

More exotic still are the Yaeyama Islands just to the north of the Tropic of Cancer. **Ishigaki** has a famous **dragon boat race** festival in May. **Taketomi** has attractive traditional houses framed by tumbling hibiscus, and star-sand beaches made from the skeletons of a myriad tiny crustacea. Jungle-covered **Iriomote** is where both the elusive **Iriomote wild cat** and the deadly **habu** (viper) live; the island is a tropical refuge fringed by coral reefs.

THE YONAGUNI PYRAMIDS

Over the past few years, divers have located trenches and platforms reminiscent of a lost city over the ocean floor between Okinawa and Yonaguni, the southernmost island in the Yaeyama group near Taiwan. There has been much speculation that these features might be man-made, or at least shaped by man at some point in the past. The discovery in 1985 of a large, sharply stepped pyramid off Yonaguni in 18m (59ft) of water heightened this speculation. Some archaeologists have tentatively dated the structure at **12,000 years** old. Some dismiss the 'man-made' theory as a fairy tale. Either way, the diving is remarkable.

Below: *Shuri-jō, which was destroyed in World War II, is once again a major tourist attraction.*

Kyūshū and Okinawa at a Glance

BEST TIMES TO VISIT

Both Kyūshū and Okinawa get most of their rainfall during the summer, when typhoons are also a risk. Spring and late autumn are the best times to visit both of these destinations, but avoid Golden Week in May. New Year is also a popular time for Japanese package tours. Yakushima is drenched by rain all year, but spring and autumn are drier.

GETTING THERE

Kyūshū: Fukuoka is well serviced by **international flights** from major Asian cities such as Seoul, Hong Kong and Bangkok. It is also connected by hydrofoil service to Pusan (Korea). **Domestic flights** service Fukuoka, Kagoshima, Kumamoto, Miyazaki, Nagasaki and Oita from all over Japan. **Ferry** links between Beppu and Shikoku are useful. **Okinawa**: Naha is serviced by a range of flights from all over Japan and international flights from Taipei and Seoul. Flights to **Ishigaki** and **Miyako-jima** also from Kansai International and Haneda. **Ferry** connections to Naha from Tokyo, Ōsaka, Kōbe, Nagoya, Hakata, Kagoshima, Miyazaki, and from Taiwan. **Yakushima** can be reached by air, **jetfoil** or ferry from Kagoshima.

GETTING AROUND

Kyūshū: The Shinkansen service from Tokyo, via Shin-Osaka or Okayama, now terminates at Hakata (**Fukuoka**), but an extension up from Kagoshima (already partially open) will be complete in 2013. A car is useful for visiting the national parks such as **Aso** and **Kirishima-Yaku** as well as coastal areas. For **Dazaifu**, take the Nishitetsu line from Nishitetsu-Fukuoka Station (30 min). For **Yanagawa**, take the JR line from Hakata Station (1 hour). **Nagasaki** has a good tram system, where a one-day pass is useful. For **Huis Ten Bosch** and Sasebo take the JR service from Nagasaki Station. For **Hirado** take either the bus from Sasebo or the boat from Kashimae through the Kujūku-shima (Ninety Nine Islands). **Imari** can be reached from Hirado or Fukuoka. Like Nagasaki, Kumamoto and Kagoshima have tram systems. **Takachiho** can be reached by bus from Kumamoto. For **Sakurajima** take a ferry from Kagoshima pier. **Okinawa**: a car is virtually essential for seeing the south and north of Okinawa Island. On the outer islands, hiring a motor scooter or bicycle is the best way to get around.

WHERE TO STAY

Fukuoka
MID-RANGE
With the Style Fukuoka, 1-9-18 Hakataeki Minami, Hakata-ku, Fukuoka-shi, tel: 92 433 3900, www.withthestyle.com/eng/index.htm Designer Ryu Kosaka has given traditional Japanese hospitality a modern spin. Outdoor swimming pool and spa; lounge bar.

Nagasaki
MID-RANGE
Baishokaku Ryokan, 2-14-1 Hamahira, Nagasaki-shi, tel: 095 824 2153. Good-sized *ryokan* hotel with an outside *onsen* with views over the city.

Kumamoto
MID-RANGE
Maruko Hotel, 11-10 Kamidori-machi Kumamoto-shi, tel: 096 353 1241. Traditional Japanese inn; basic, comfortable rooms. Indoor *onsen*, small outside hot tub.

Takachiho
BUDGET
Folkcraft Ryokan Kaminoya, 806-5 Mitai, Takachiho-chō, Miyazaki Prefecture, tel: 0982 72 2111. Good location for the gorge and evening dance performances.

Beppu
BUDGET
Yokoso, Kannawa Ida 3-kumi, Beppu-shi, tel: 0977 66 0440. Basic but clean and very well priced (you pay extra for air conditioning). Cooking equipment available free.

Okinawa
Okinawa Island is geared towards big, beach resort hotels. Accommodation on the outer islands ranges from *minshuku* to simpler hotels.

BUDGET

Nitta-sou Minshuku, Taketomi Island, tel: 0980 85 2201. Traditional inn where ox-drawn carts trundle past.

Naha
MID-RANGE

Naha Central Hotel, 2-16-36 Makishi (behind Mitsukoshi), tel: 098 862 6070, fax: 862 6109. Good value, *onsen*, well located for shopping.

WHERE TO EAT

Fukuoka
Try the Nagahama *ramen* (noodles cooked with pork stock) – just pick the most appetizing looking stand from the hundreds along this famous street on the edge of the docks.

Nagasaki
Chinatown has a huge selection of restaurants serving *chanpon* (noodles with seafood and vegetables). Shinbashi Gourmet Street is not surprisingly a good bet for both nightlife and food. Also visit the oldest Western-style restaurant in Japan, the Tenjin Coffeehouse, in Glover Gardens.

Gohan, 2-32 Aburayamachi, Nagasaki, tel: 095 825 3600. Traditional sushi restaurant in lovely setting.

Kumamoto
The streets south of the station have a big range of bars and restaurants.

Ichinosōko, 2-8 Kachikōji, (off Kami-tōri). Old warehouse con-

verted into tasteful beer house. Serves mostly light meals.

Kagoshima
Satsuma-aji, 6-29 Higashi Sengoku-chō (off Tenmonkan-dōri). The best place for *Satsuma-age*.

TOURS AND EXCURSIONS

Kyūshū
Yanagawa: one-hour boat trips along the canals begin close to the Nishitetsu Yanagawa Stn. **Sakurajima**: a JR sightseeing bus tours the island twice daily. Free to JR pass holders.

Okinawa
Naha Kōtsu, tel: 098 868 3750. Arranges day trips to South Okinawa's battle sites. **Fathoms Diving**, Chatan-Cho, Miyagi 1-64, 3 F Seajoy Bldg, Okinawa, tel: 090 8766 0868, www.fathoms.net PADI instruction, dive excursions (including Yonaguni Pyramids). **Whale-watching Association**, tel: 098 987 2277. Organizes boat trips out of Zamami in season, from January to March.

USEFUL CONTACTS

Kyūshū
Fukuoka
Tourist Information Centre (Hakata Station), tel: 092 431

3003. Get the Fukuoka City Visitor's Guide here.
Eki Rent-a-car, tel: 092 431 8775.

Nagasaki Prefectural Tourist Federation (2F opposite Nagasaki Station), tel: 095 826 9407, for information on Nagasaki Prefecture.
Kagoshima
Eki Rent-a-car, tel: 099 258 1412
Kumamoto
Eki Rent-a-car, tel: 096 352 4313.

Okinawa
Naha
Okinawa Tourist, tel: 098 862 1111. Can help with arrangements for tours of the outer islands.

Nippon Rent-a-car, tel: 098 868 4554. Offices both at the airport and downtown.
Ryūkyū Kaiun, tel: 098 868 1126. Ferry reservations to mainland Japan.

Ryūkyū Air Commuter (RAC) and **Japan Transocean Airways (JTA)**, tel: 098 869 8522, or toll-free: 0120 10 0359. For inter-island services (RAC) and flights from regional cities (JTA).

Adventist Medical Centre, tel: 098 946 2833, www.amc.gr.jp Has English-speaking staff.

KAGOSHIMA	J	F	M	A	M	J	J	A	S	O	N	D
AVERAGE TEMP. °C	7	8	11	16	20	23	27	28	25	20	15	9
AVERAGE TEMP. °F	45	46	52	61	68	73	81	82	77	68	59	48
RAINFALL mm	87	103	161	230	259	400	304	213	216	106	88	71
RAINFALL in	3.4	4.1	6.3	9.1	10.2	15.8	12.0	8.4	8.5	4.2	3.5	2.8
DAYS OF RAINFALL	5	8	16	9	6	18	13	21	16	6	6	6

Travel Tips

Tourist Information

Japan National Tourist Organization (JNTO) has twelve overseas offices and an excellent general website at www.jnto.go.jp
UK: Heathcoat House, 20 Savile Row, London W1X 1AE, tel: 020 7734 4290, fax: 7734 4290. See www.seejapan.co.uk for map and brochure requests.
USA: One Rockefeller Plaza, Suite 1250, New York, NY 10020, tel: 212 757 5640, fax: 307 6754. See www.japan travelinfo.com **Other offices:** Bangkok, Beijing, Frankfurt, Hong Kong, Los Angeles, Paris, San Francisco, Seoul, Sydney, Toronto.
JNTO Tourist Information Centre (TIC) in Tokyo has English-speaking staff and a huge range of maps/leaflets. Narita and Kansai International airports also have TICs (see At a Glance sections). Virtually all train stations have information centres inside or next door, usually marked '**?**'. English-speaking staff are hard to come by outside the major cities. Also, information tends to be strictly local, but maps/leaflets are always useful.

JNTO runs a **Japan Travel-Phone** service toll-free (09:00–17:00, daily) on 0088 22 4800. English-speaking operators can provide language assistance and travel information. In Tokyo call the TIC.

Entry Requirements

Japan has reciprocal visa exemption arrangements with around 60 countries including the UK, Canada, Republic of Ireland, USA and New Zealand. Citizens of these countries entering Japan on holiday or business can stay for 90 days without a visa (Irish and UK citizens can apply for an extension of another 90 days when they are in Japan). Citizens of **South Africa** need tourist visas. For full visa information, check the Ministry of Foreign Affairs website at: www.mofa.go.jp or ask your local Japanese embassy. If spending more than 90 days, foreigners must register and carry an Alien Registration Card. As of 1 July 2007, when entering Japan you are requested to hand in a Customs Declaration form of both your accompanied and unaccom-

panied baggage at the Customs Clearance. Forms are available on the plane/ship or at the Customs office.

Customs

The **duty-free allowance** for **non-residents** (over 20) is 400 cigarettes or 250g of tobacco (or a 500g combination), three 760ml bottles of alcohol and 57g (2 oz) of perfume, plus up to ¥200,000 of gifts and souvenirs. Any amount of currency may be brought into the country. Prohibited items include firearms and pornographic material.
Illegal drugs in particular are not tolerated, as Paul McCartney once found to his cost; jail is not part of any recommended itinerary in Japan. Quarantine regulations ban the import of plants, fresh fruits, raw meat, etc.

Health Requirements

There are no special health or vaccination requirements for entering Japan.

Getting There

By Air: A range of European, US and Asian airlines all fly daily to Narita (Tokyo International Airport). From London, JAL flies non-stop to Kansai International Airport. From the USA, Continental Airlines, JAL and Northwest do so too. Asian carriers offer the most flights to regional airports in Japan. Aeroflot flies from Vladivostok to Niigata.

By Ferry: There is a twice monthly ferry service from Vladivostok to Niigata, or to Fushiki near Toyama (Jul–Sep). From Pusan in Korea there is a daily hydrofoil service to Fukuoka and a less frequent ferry service to Fukuoka and Shimonoseki. From Shanghai there are ferries to Kōbe or Ōsaka and from Keelung (Taiwan) to Naha, Okinawa.

What to Pack

Plenty of changes of **light cotton** clothing and an **umbrella** are essential in summer. **Comfortable clothes for sitting on *tatami*** are also important. A mixture of layers is useful at all other times, plus a warm coat in winter. The Japanese tend to dress smartly (whether formal or casual). Err on the side of caution at classy restaurants or hotels. **Slip-on shoes** are very useful, as temples, shrines, *tatami* rooms anywhere and ordinary homes are shoe-free zones. Hole-free socks or tights avoid toe-curling embarrassment in traditional restaurants or *ryokan*. A small **dictionary** (with romanized spellings of Japanese words and *kanji*) may help you out of difficulty in more remote areas. Rail stations have many flights of steps and there is virtually no space on trains for big suitcases. Keep your luggage **light** if you plan on doing a lot of travelling.

Money Matters

Currency: The yen comes in ¥1, ¥5, ¥10, ¥50, ¥100 and ¥500 coins, ¥1,000, ¥2,000 ¥5,000 and ¥10,000 notes.
Exchange: Japan's banking system is cumbersome. **Cash is king.** Keep the yen equivalent of several hundred dollars or pounds on you. The low crime rate means this is not as crazy as it sounds. **American Express** and **Visa** are widely accepted, but by no means do all hotels, shops and restaurants accept credit cards – particularly outside the major cities. **Traveller's cheques** can be exchanged at all major banks (open 09:00–15.00, Mon–Fri; foreign exchange desks do not always open at 09:00), but be prepared to wait. Most **Post Offices** (09:00–17:00, Mon–Fri) and major hotels will change major currencies. **Citibank ATMs** (often open 24 hours) give cash advances on foreign-issued cards such as Visa and Mastercard. So do ATMs at Post Offices with the International ATM green-clover symbol.
Tipping: This is an alien concept in Japan. Service charges are usually incorporated in the bill. Do not tip taxi drivers, and restaurant or hotel staff.
Consumption Tax: A 5% tax is charged on all goods and services, sometimes inclusive of the quoted price and sometimes exclusive. A local tax of 3% is added to hotel bills over ¥15,000 per night and over ¥7,500 per person in restaurants. This may make it cheaper not to charge all meals to your room bill.

Accommodation

Western-style accommodation is normally charged on a **room-only** basis. **Japanese-style** accommodation is on a **per person basis** and includes breakfast and dinner.
Luxury: (¥20,000 upwards). A night in a **top *ryokan*** (Japanese inn) with *kaiseki-ryōri* in *tatami* rooms (sleeping 2–4 people) and a beautiful garden setting can cost over ¥70,000 per person. Any *ryokan* will have communal baths for men and women, which is all part of the experience. **Top Western-style hotels** costing ¥20,000 plus per night or more offer all first-class amenities.
Mid-range: (¥8–20,000). Second-tier *ryokan* range from around ¥12,000 at the lower end to ¥20,000 (or more) for an

---

Useful Phrases

Ohayō-gozaimasu • Good morning
Konnichi-wa • Good day
Komban-wa • Good evening
Sumimasen • Excuse me (to get attention)
Hai • Yes
Wakarimasen • I don't understand
Dōzo • Please (when offering something)
O negai shimasu • Please (when requesting something)
Dōmo arigatō-gozaimasu • Thank you very much
Dōmo • Thanks
Kampai! • Cheers!
Eigo ga dekimasu ka? • Can you speak English?
Ikura desu ka? • How much does it cost?

en-suite room. In country locations, **Pensions** are a good option (guest houses, two meals included). **Shukubō** (temple lodgings) at centres such as Kōya San offer simple accommodation and vegetarian food, but are not always cheap. **Business hotels** offer a solid, if often soulless Western option for the independent traveller, ranging from ¥8–15,000 (no meals). Generally reliable chains include the Daiichi, Tōkyū and Washington groups. **Budget:** (Under ¥8000 per person). *Ryokan* in this price bracket (some have a no-meal option) provide perfectly good accommodation. A cheaper option still is the *minshuku*, a no-frills family-run *ryokan*. **Capsule hotels**, originally aimed at incapacitated businessmen, have coffin-like rooms with all amenities; they are not for the claustrophobic, and rarely used by women. If you are completely stuck, **love hotels** can be good value for an overnight stay (not their intended purpose). **Cheaper business hotels** (¥5–7000) are clean, if sometimes shabby,

and provide *yukata*, toothbrush and shampoo. **Youth Hostels** are cheap. Some are well located, but beware of school brigades rising at the crack of dawn. Contact your local YH organization or JNTO for details (which can also tell you about camping). **Reservations:** reserve well ahead at major destinations, particularly for weekends and public holidays such as New Year, Golden Week (first week of May), August and in spring and autumn. Top hotels have English-speaking staff. Elsewhere try and get a Japanese speaker to reserve for you. Tourist Information Centres can make bookings on the spot if you want to keep your itinerary flexible. The following services are useful for making reservations from overseas:
www.japaneseguesthouses.com is a highly informative site, useful for booking luxury and budget *ryokans*, including several recommended in this guide. At the budget end, for *ryokans* and small hotels try the **Welcome Inn Reservation Centre**, www.itcj.or.jp

Eating Out

Japan has a massive range of international cuisine. You will rarely be short of a pizza if raw fish is not your thing. Reliable **restaurant chains** include Cappriciosa (massive Italian portions), Volks (steak) and Skylark (family food). Starbucks and Doutor coffee shops are ubiquitous.
The Japanese eat early: lunch starts from 11:30 and dinner from 18:00. If you cannot stomach the idea of a local breakfast (rice, raw egg, seaweed and fish), try a coffee shop. The **teishoku** (a set meal of 2–3 dishes, miso soup and rice) is the non-Japanese speaker's godsend. Here is a brief guide to some different kinds of eating and drinking establishments:
izakaya – informal, noisy restaurants serving range of dishes such as *yakitori*.
aka-chōchin – type of *izakaya*, red lanterns hanging outside.
kissaten – coffee shop usually serving *mōningu setto* breakfast (toast, egg, coffee).
nomiya – bar with counter; regulars keep their own bottles.
robataya – serves rustic-style charcoal-grilled food (the preparation of which is often a theatrical performance).
ryōtei – elegant, expensive restaurant serving *kaiseki-ryōri*.
shokudō – convenient, inexpensive. Order from plastic food models in the window.
sushiya – sit at the counter and choose your sushi or order a *teishoku*. *Kaiten-zushi* is sushi on a conveyor belt.
yatai – outdoor stalls cooking simple dishes. Can be good.

CONVERSION TABLE		
FROM	**TO**	**MULTIPLY BY**
Millimetres	Inches	0.0394
Metres	Yards	1.0936
Metres	Feet	3.281
Kilometres	Miles	0.6214
Square kilometres	Square miles	0.386
Hectares	Acres	2.471
Litres	Pints	1.760
Kilograms	Pounds	2.205
Tonnes	Tons	0.984
To convert Celsius to Fahrenheit: x 9 ÷ 5 + 32		

Transport

Air: This is the quickest and most convenient method for one-off trips to Hokkaidō and Kyūshū in particular. Air travel is **price competitive** with rail transport on most major routes. Airlines can be contacted on the following toll-free numbers inside Japan: JAL, tel: 0120 02 9222; ANA, tel: 0120 25 5971; JAS, tel: 0120 51 1283.
Rail: Japan's rail system is the best in the world. Japan Rail (JR) runs six major regional networks. Private companies operate several others. If you are planning on more than one return journey from Tokyo to Kyoto, buy a **Japan Rail Pass** (www.japanrailpass.net) from JAL, JTB or other agents *before you leave for Japan*. An exchange voucher for a one-, two- or three-week JR Pass for ordinary or Green Car (first-class) use can only be purchased **outside Japan by temporary visitors**. On arrival, exchange the voucher at a JR Travel Service Centre. The JR Pass is valid on all JR trains except the *Nozomi* (Super-Express) Shinkansen. Rail Pass holders can make **seat reservations** at no extra cost. This makes sense at busy periods or to ensure a non-smoking seat. English timetables, available from JNTO, provide adequate reference for most routes. Go to the *midori no madoguchi* (Green Window Counter) at any rail station with the number of the train you want to catch, date and destination (preferably written down). Luggage lockers are handy for

lightening your load, but can only be used for up to three days. The **JR East Infoline**, tel: 03 3423 0111, open 10:00–18:00, Mon–Fri, is an English-language information service for nationwide train enquiries.
Shinkansen (bullet trains) run on six different lines. The *Kodama* stops at all Tōkaidō line stations; the *Hikari* at major stations, and the *Nozomi* (reserved seats only) only seven times between Tokyo and Hakata (Kyūshū), a journey of around five hours. Individual tickets are subject to a Shinkansen surcharge.
Tokkyū (limited express trains) also require a surcharge but seats can be reserved. **Kaisoku** (rapid trains) have no surcharge. **Futsū** (ordinary trains) stop at every station.
Buses: Long-distance bus services are cheaper than rail, but are no match for speed or comfort.
Car hire: A car is an asset in remote areas and not very expensive for a group of four. Keep the cost down by avoiding expressways (tolls are exorbitant). Use Shōbunsha's bilingual *Japan Road Atlas*. Japan drives on the left and road signs are written in both *kanji* and Roman letters. The top speed limit is 100km/h (62.5mph) on expressways and 80km/h (50mph) on metropolitan highways. To hire a car you need an International Driver's Licence as well as your own national licence. Cars can be rented at airports and stations from most internationally known operators. **Eki** (**Station**) **Rent-a-car** has some good deals

combining train and car hire (*see* At a Glance sections).
Ferry: Even though bridges and tunnels now join all four main islands, there are ferry services from Honshū across the **Inland Sea** to Kyūshū and Shikoku as well as north to Hokkaidō.

Business Hours

Shops are open from 10:00–19:00, including Sundays. Most close one day a week. Convenience stores such as Seven Eleven operate 24 hours. **Museums** tend to close on Mondays and at New Year. If a public holiday falls on a Monday, many shut the following day instead. Always check local listings before making a special trip. The last admission is usually 30 minutes before closing.

Time Difference

Japan is 9 hours ahead of Greenwich Mean Time (GMT).

Communications

Telephone services in Japan are expensive, but getting cheaper. Pre-paid phone cards (terefon kādo) for public telephones can be bought from vending machines or newspaper kiosks. Cards valid for international calls (*kokusai denwa*) come in ¥1000, ¥3000 and ¥5000 units. Use them in grey pay phones marked 'ISDN' or 'international'. Remember your overseas mobile probably won't work in Japan. Companies such as Rentafone Japan (www.rentafonejapan.com) hire out phones for short-term use while in the country. **Fax** facilities are available at top hotels, post offices and convenience stores. **Public Internet** access has become much easier. In many cities there are growing numbers of cyber-cafés and access is always possible at Kinko's business stores – at a price.

Electricity

Japan operates on a 100V current. Plugs are of the flat, two-pin variety. A transformer must be used for overseas appliances.

Weights and Measures

Japan uses the metric system, but retains some quirks of its own like the *tsubo* (3.954 sq yards), used to measure area.

Health Precautions

Tap water is safe to drink, if not very palatable. Despite past outbreaks of E. coli food poisoning, Japan is generally a safe place to eat. Mosquitoes can be a nuisance in summer, but malaria is not an issue. A comparatively high percentage of Japanese are carriers of Hepatitis B, which is more of a problem than HIV. Japan is a condom-friendly society. Four decades after the rest of the world, the contraceptive pill has finally been given approval, but bring your own supplies.

Personal Safety

The crime rate in Japan is very low. You are more likely to have a lost item returned to you than have anything stolen. However, take all sensible precautions and lock up any bicycle you rent. The incidence of rape is low (it is also probably underreported). In general, it is safe for women to walk on their own at night. The most common complaint is 'groping' on crowded commuter trains; a stamp on the foot com-

bined with verbal abuse can work wonders.

Emergencies

The telephone emergency service number for the **fire brigade** or an **ambulance** is **119**. For the **police**, it is **110**, but do not expect assistance in English. In an emergency try the toll-free 24-hour English-speaking Jhelp.com tel: 0120 46 1997. A general information number is 03 3501 0110 (Japanese/English).

Etiquette

The Japanese will forgive you just about anything for being foreign, but some basic rules will help avoid real faux pas:
• Take a name or business card with you and treat business cards from others with respect (do not doodle on them).
• The Japanese give their surname first (as does this book). It is polite to always add *San* to a name, e.g. Suzuki *San*. (Mr, Mrs, or Miss Suzuki)
• Always be prepared to remove your shoes.
• Stay cool under trying circumstances. Losing your temper gets you nowhere.

GOOD READING

Bird, Isabella (1984) *Unbeaten Tracks in Japan*, Virago.
Crowell, Todd (2002) *Tokyo: City on the Edge*, Asia 2000.
Dower, John (1999) *Embracing Defeat*, Penguin.
Hearn, Lafcadio (1984) *Writings from Japan*, Penguin.
Kayano, Shigeru (1994) *Our Land was a Forest*, Westview Press.
MacFarlane, Alan (2008) *Japan Through the Looking Glass*.
Schlesinger, Jacob (1997) *Shadow Shōguns*, Simon and Schuster.
Seidensticker, Edward (1983) *Low City, High City*, Tuttle.
Williamson, Kate T (2004) *A Year in Japan*.
Yoshimoto, Banana (1997) *Amrita*, Faber and Faber.

INDEX

Note: Numbers in **bold** indicate photographs